Quarry Land

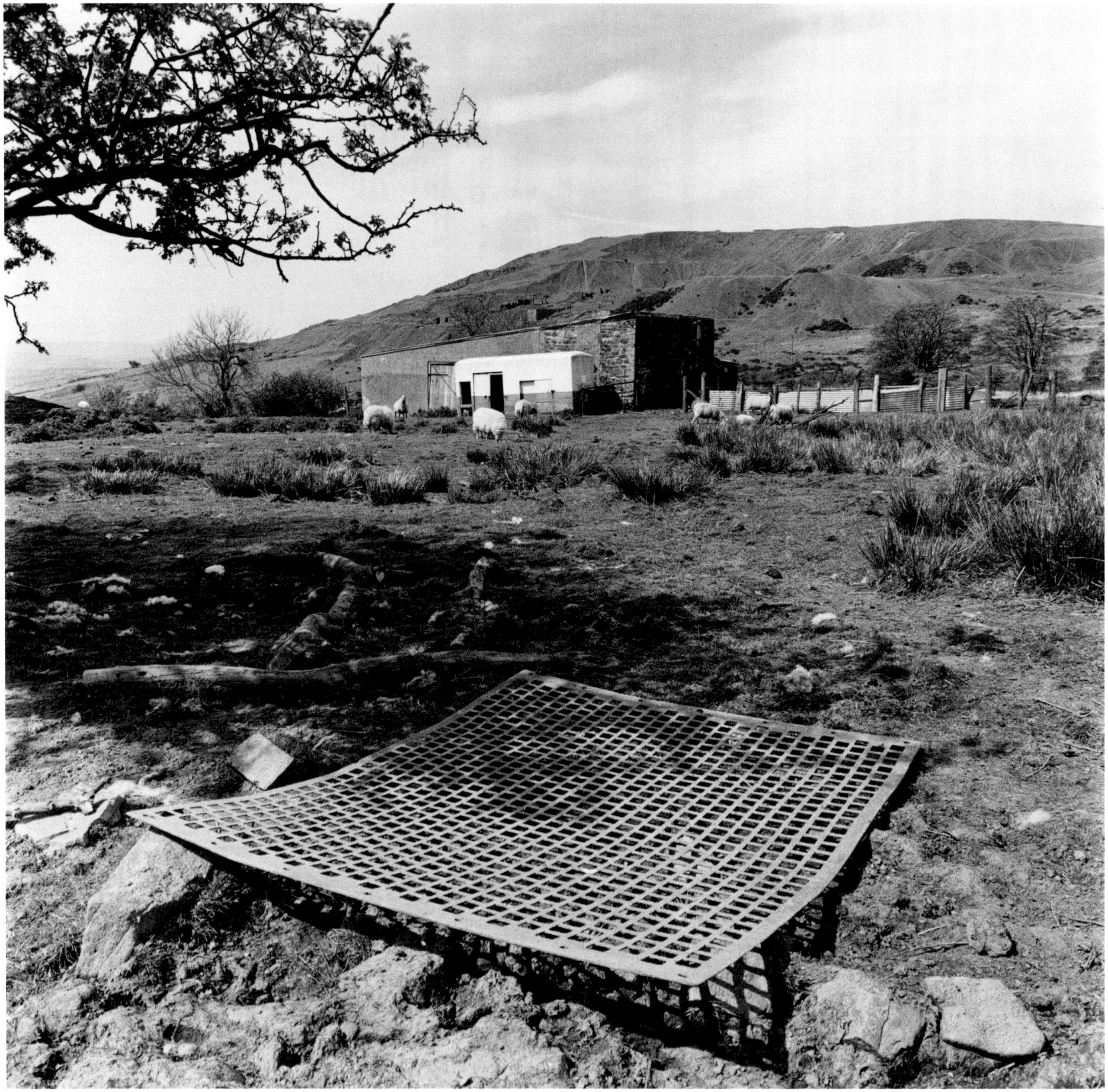

1 | Sheep sheds with iron grille and abandoned quarries, Titterstone Clee

Quarry Land
Impermanent Landscapes of the Clee Hills

Simon Denison
Foreword by Paul Hill

Greyscale Books

'Everything is in a state of flux. Nothing remains the same'
Heraclitus

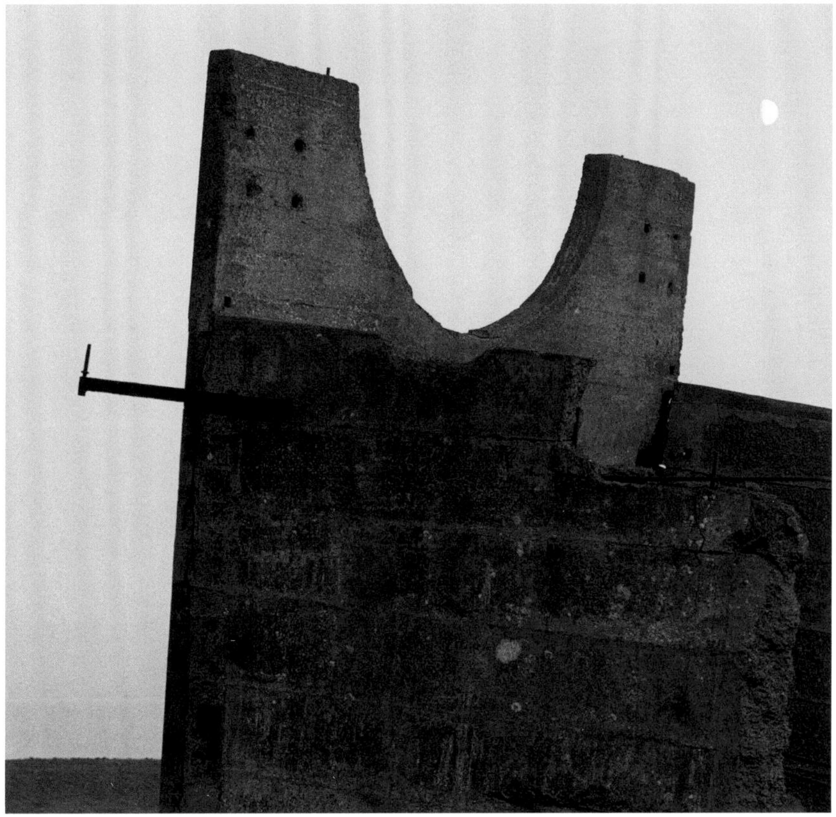

2 | Ruined quarry building, Titterstone Clee

Foreword

Paul Hill

I frequently walk from my Derbyshire home to a high crag (1,200 feet) two miles away that, on a clear day, affords a magnificent panoramic view of the Peak District to the north and east, the Midland Plain to the south, and the just discernible hills of my home county Shropshire to the west. On exceptional days I can definitely see the unique outline of the Wrekin and, with powerful binoculars, I am sure I can just make out the Clee Hills 60 miles to the south west. But maybe that is wishful thinking on my part. I would love it to be true as they were an iconic backdrop to my childhood in Ludlow where I was born in 1941.

I spent a great deal of time in those years playing on the town's Whitcliffe Hill above the River Teme. From that fern strewn vantage point you have, in my opinion, the finest view in England with the glorious Ludlow Castle and St Laurence's Church in the foreground and the distinctive shape of the Clee Hills in the distance.

These uplands became the goals for many an adventure. With my friend Phil who, like me, became a journalist later in life (he worked for the BBC on *Today* and *The World at One*), I would see how far I could cycle up the frighteningly steep Angel Bank on the Ludlow to Cleobury Mortimer road without dismounting. At the top, at Clee Hill village, we would look down on Ludlow, Leominster and Tenbury Wells prior to putting on an extra pullover for the death-defying and high-speed descent back to Ludlow before it got dark.

The village of Clee Hill seemed an isolated outpost then and we hardly ever saw anyone on those cycle trips. The impression I get from Simon Denison's beautifully melancholic images of the area is that it is a lonely place to live in even today.

Phil and I have only recently met up again for the first time in well over 40 years and we talked about those childhood adventures as if they took place only yesterday. I have very few photographs of those times, but the ones I do have are precious evocations of pleasurable companionship, warm summers, empty roads, and no responsibilities.

A few years later I got seriously interested in photography, and in 1965 became a freelance photojournalist after six years as a newspaper reporter. By this time I was married, and was based in Wolverhampton. My happy childhood was recalled on fleeting visits to Shropshire, but that post-war period was one that I always felt I needed to mark in some way. I wondered if photography could help me recapture those times, or at least describe the locations of those memories.

Would my interpretations be any different to those made by thousands of other photographers? Photographs are brilliant at showing us places and things, but can they *say* or express anything about the maker's past life? Can a photograph transcend the information recorded by the camera?

So I went back to Shropshire in the second half of the 1960s to see if I could reflect a *feeling* of the place that was so integral to my childhood. The view of the Clee Hills from Whitcliffe seemed the same, as did Ludlow cattle market, the smithy, the baker's kitchen, the coal-yard, the cinema, my old school, and the narrow streets and passageways. The gritty black and white prints I made gave them an artificial patina of age. They could have been made in the 1940s. They were quite 'good' photographs, but they did not match up to my memories. True, I had created a recognisable spirit of the place, but the images said more about my relationship to the medium at that period of my career than they did about my childhood. But I'll settle for that. They evoked a particular place, a particular time, and a particular photographic style – and they were exhibited and published too, much to my satisfaction and surprise.

In a similar way, the topography of South Shropshire has become an integral part of Simon Denison's life. He has lived in the area for nearly as long as I did all those years ago, and although not a local man the Clee Hills have become a magnet and a muse for him. He has worked hard and long

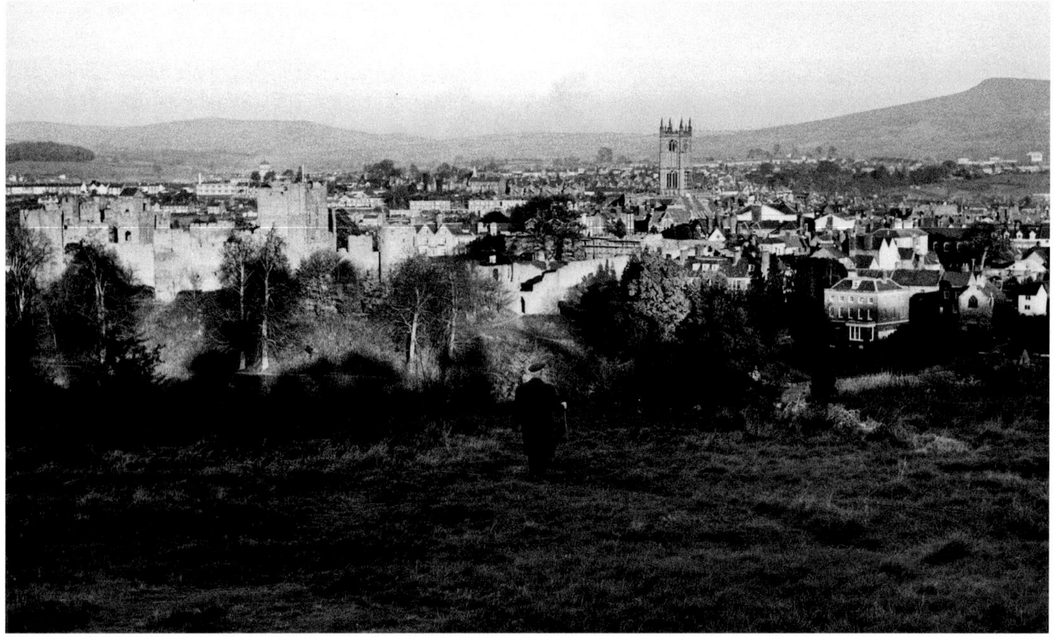

View from Whitcliffe, Ludlow, 1969 (Paul Hill) – Brown Clee background left, Titterstone Clee back right

to reflect his relationship to this fascinating area. Not for him the easy pictorialist clichés that will offend no one. He walks into his subject matter via his back door, like me. And it is this sense of intimacy with the landscape that is such a telling feature of this book. The moods of different seasons, weather conditions and of the photographer are exquisitely revealed through finely crafted black and white photographs. Each picture is part of a personal narrative – pieces that contribute to a satisfying whole.

The Clee Hills are largely man-altered in a contemporary as well as in an historical sense, so it is most appropriate that he has included interviews with local residents and workers. This has enabled him to give us an extra and engaging documentation of the area, and the opportunity to show another photographic skill – portraiture.

Simon Denison's metaphoric vision of the Clees is one that is full of industrial remnants and abandoned objects. The impression is of a harsh and unforgiving landscape – a place forgotten, overlooked, and apart. The work is beautifully elegiac. Other photographers will give you a technicolor, sanitised, Heritage Britain vision of this landscape. But Simon's pictures say more about a place that I only have two tangible mementoes of – snapshots taken by a stranger of Phil and me in Clee Hill village over 50 years ago. Now, I have this book to stir my memories, to enjoy for its photographs, and to learn from the stories of its residents what a unique part of England this is. But then I suppose I always knew that a place so hard to get to as a youngster, but so beautiful to contemplate from a distance, must be special.

Paul Hill, MBE
De Montfort University, Leicester

Introduction

Simon Denison

The first time that I climbed to the summit of Brown Clee, the higher of the two Clee Hills in Shropshire and the highest point in the English Midlands, was on the morning of the new millennium – 1st January 2000. I had lived on the lower flanks of the hill for a couple of years, but for one reason or another had never yet made it to the very top. This seemed like an auspicious day to take a bird's-eye view of the lie of the land.

Not yet knowing the best route, I struggled up the steep north shoulder of the hill, following what I thought was a footpath but which soon vanished under a thick crop of shin-tugging bracken. Before long the multiple-dished telecoms mast on the summit came into view, set among spoilheaps on the far side of a stretch of brown heather-covered bog. There was nothing remotely pretty about the hilltop itself, but the surrounding views were satisfying enough, with distant hills receding in all directions.

Not long after I reached the mast, the cloud dropped and the summit was shrouded in whiteness. Opting for an easier path down I followed a tarmac road, used by telecoms engineers, which led down a steep former incline railway line through a plantation of conifers. On either side of the road at the top of the hill were deep quarry pits, just visible in the fog, grassed-over spoilheaps and the gaunt ruins of former quarry buildings – a stone crusher, a tarmac plant, a locomotive shed and other structures, all roofless, their reinforced concrete frames gaping open at the sky like primed mantraps. The sense of desolation was chilling.

It was also a revelation. I had no idea of the existence of these remains on the top of my own hill. Industrial ruins are generally not tourist sights – unlike, say, the ruins of medieval castles or abbeys – and the remains on Brown Clee are neither listed in guidebooks nor signposted from the road. Even the footpaths up the hill are poorly marked. These ruins are rarely discussed, and they remain largely unknown, forgotten, I suspect, even by local people.

This moves me, because it means that an entire episode of large-scale human intervention in the landscape is drifting into oblivion. Men and women came here, set up buildings and machinery, blasted out massive pits, broke stone, laboured for much of their lives. Many were injured by flying stone shards, some were killed. From the end of the 19th century to the middle of the 20th, this was a place of activity and noise, with the pounding of the crusher and the clattering of the railway trucks. Eventually the quarries closed, the railway was dismantled, the buildings collapsed, and the spoilheaps grassed over. The hilltop reverted to silence. Given a bit more time, the visible ruins will disappear altogether, leaving nothing but buried traces for archaeologists to pick over.

When I climbed Brown Clee that day, I was already involved in photographing man-made features of the rural landscape. For my book *The Human Landscape*, I made images across Britain of functional everyday structures – typically derelict or abandoned – which seemed to symbolise the ubiquity but also the transience of human impact on the land. A few of my early photographs from the Clee Hills made it into that collection (they are marked by an asterisk in this book).

But as I looked out over the bleak terrain at the top of the hill, it struck me that the Clee Hills provided everything that I had been seeking elsewhere – a metaphor, in landscape, for the passage of time and the impermanence of human endeavour. The realisation mirrored a process that often happens when I am taking photographs. I can be struggling with an image, framing and reframing it, hunting for a way to make the image speak, until I give up, take the camera off the tripod and turn around. And there I find the really telling image. It was lying right behind me all along.

South Shropshire is a landscape of wooded, pastoral hills, and from any distance Brown Clee appears no different from any of the other hills in the surrounding region. Only the overgrown concrete footings of the old limestone works at Cockshutford [10], a tiny hamlet halfway up the hill, provide a clue to the industrial character of the hill's twin summits, known as Abdon Burf (540m) and Clee Burf (510m). Thickly forested on its eastern side, with open grazing to the west, the hill can only be reached via several miles of single-track roads through small, red-sandstone villages and fields of grazing sheep.

The landscape around Brown Clee seems the epitome of remote 'unspoiled' English countryside, and it is almost impossible now to imagine the din and bustle of the area in the early decades of the 20th century. Abdon was once known locally as the 'miners' village' because of the number of inhabitants engaged in that industry, but it is now no more than a tiny farming hamlet. I must have driven through the village over a hundred times without ever seeing a single person on the road or working in adjacent fields [40, 41].

Nothing could be more different than the atmosphere around Titterstone Clee, Brown Clee's southern neighbour. Despite being the lower of the two hills by a few metres, it is far better known and is often referred to simply as 'Clee Hill'. Titterstone has a more distinctive shape than Brown Clee, its peak (533m) crowned by golf-ball and mushroom radars visible from at least ten miles away in almost every direction [16].

Titterstone is also more accessible than Brown Clee. The main road east from South Shropshire's market town, Ludlow – heading to Worcester, Birmingham and beyond – runs up over the southern flank of the hill, and it is possible to drive right to the summit, past anomalous red-brick Victorian terraces built for quarry workers at Dhustone [22], to a pot-holed car park set amid spoilheaps and ruined quarry buildings at the top.

Titterstone is industrial to the core, and doesn't try to hide it. Coal mining and quarrying were carried out here more extensively, and for much longer, than on Brown Clee, and the hill's windswept, virtually treeless plateau is scarred everywhere by spoilheaps and slagheaps, capped shafts, old quarries, pitted dirt roads and the derelict remains of industrial buildings. The little settlement of Dhustone even takes its name from the type of stone quarried on the hill.

Most of the industrial remains date from the 19th and 20th centuries but, as on Brown Clee, medieval and post-medieval coal mining 'bell-pits' – so-called because of the shape they take on following collapse – bear witness to the length of the industrial history of the two hills.

Indeed, the Clee Hills are the only English hills marked on the late 13th century *Mappa Mundi*, Britain's earliest world map, attesting no doubt to the national importance of their minerals even then. The map is now housed in Hereford Cathedral, some 30 miles south of the Clee Hills, but historians think it was probably made on the other side of the country in Lincolnshire. On one part of Titterstone, quarrying continues to the present day in a large pit, Clee Hill Quarry, managed by Hanson plc (formerly by ARC). Its towering crusher buildings are visible from the main road over the hill.

At the highest point of the road stands Clee Hill village, a settlement that grew with the quarries in the early decades of the 20th century. With its non-local, semi-urban style of architecture, the village looks like it could belong to almost any industrialised area of Britain [19]. It is a striking anomaly within the wider local landscape. Clee Hill people have always held themselves apart, until fairly recently speaking a unique dialect, and even now tending to stay in the village where they were born. Elsewhere in Shropshire, Clee Hill has a reputation for being a bit rough, largely undeserved no doubt, but not helped by the litter of burnt-out cars and caravans that seem a constant feature of the muddy former quarry railway line at the back of the village and among the spoilheaps a short distance uphill [24, 27].

Clee Hill lies only four miles from Ludlow, one of the favoured new destinations for downshifting city-dwellers with idealised expectations of rural England. And there is no doubt that many local people, and not just the incomers, regard Titterstone as a bit of an eyesore, somehow frightening with its industrial ruins, unkempt boggy plateau and endless winter fogs. Yet for me, this quality of desertion is what lends Titterstone its powerful appeal. As on neighbouring Brown Clee, the atmosphere of a place where time has moved on is almost tangible – the hill is cloaked in the kind of echoing silence that enfolds you when the circus has left town.

The absence of other people is one of the defining characteristics of a visit to either of the Clee Hills. In all the times I have walked the hills with my camera, I have rarely met more than one other walker, maybe a couple, or occasionally someone on horseback. Just as often, I see no one at all.

But what you do find on the Clee Hills are the traces of people who have been there not long before, but have since moved on. You come across piles of logs left by forestry workers on Brown Clee, or 'Keep Out' signs on Titterstone shot up by local lads with air rifles [20, 21], or burnt-out cars tipped into the old quarry pools or hollows [29, 30], or the remains of campfires near the summits of each hill – each one of these marks on the landscape surviving a short while after the people who made them have gone, but each one itself destined to be swept away in time.

One afternoon, I photographed an unwanted caravan tucked into a fold between spoilheaps above Clee Hill village [26]. Six months later it was smashed to pieces by vandals. A fragile sheep shed on Brown Clee, banged together out of corrugated iron fixed to the wheelbase of an old quarry cart, must have survived in that state for years by the time I approached it one September day with my camera [35]. The following winter it was blown apart in New Year gales.

But if none of these structures lasts forever, at least some man-made features of the landscape are replaced when they rot away. The 'tree-post' near Random Farm on Titterstone, known locally as the 'Three-Forked Pole', supposedly marks the meeting point of three parishes on the top of the hill. Every 30 years or so the pole decays and a new one is put in its place. No one knows when the first pole was erected although photographs record one early replacement ceremony in the 1920s. The pole is said to be a magnet for walkers with some knowledge of the hill, but I have never yet seen anyone near it; only a slow-moving hill pony that came to inspect what was going on when I erected my tripod there, and turned its head to the side in a magnificent gesture of indifference just as I depressed the shutter release [31].

The history of human intervention in the landscape of the Clee Hills begins, of course, long before the industrial and medieval periods, and one of the earliest structures to survive is the Iron Age hillfort of Nordy Bank on Brown Clee, its deep ditches and grassed-over ramparts eerily foreshadowing the quarry pits and spoilheaps that would be created elsewhere on the Clee Hills some 2,500 years later [33].

When we think of historic remains, we tend to think first of this type of ancient monument or of ruined buildings – as if only the most permanent type of man-made structure qualifies as worthy of record. But often I find more ephemeral remains more evocative as symbols of the passage of time. Take the tatty white signpost at the top of Brown Clee's former incline railway, no longer carrying any form of notice, mute now, its paint flaking into the grass [36]. What did the sign say? What warning or instruction did it once give? Nobody that I have asked has any idea. Its purpose has been served and yet the signpost remains.

Equally moving, for me, is the stand of mature chestnut trees now swamped by the conifers of Brown Clee's commercial forest. Once these trees stood in open air by a stone field wall at the edge of a pasture. Now, as one era has been overtaken by another, their twisting limbs reach up out of their conifer prison towards the only light they have left – a tiny window that lies directly overhead [38].

Sometimes the most evocative landscapes are those – like battlefields, for instance – where a traumatic event has happened that has left no trace, just memories echoing in the silence. At the summit of Brown Clee lie a number of strangely picturesque pools, still waters with tiny boating jetties, fringed by reeds with a backdrop of deciduous trees. Under the still surface of one of them, Boyne Water, lies the engine of a World War II bomber that hit the ground in fog, bounced, and plunged into the pool; one of several aircraft, both Allied and German, that crashed on the hill. The engine was never dredged out and lies there still, entombed in mud [49].

If the landscapes of the Clee Hills evoke a sense of the brevity of life, it is because everywhere, sadly, they contain the signs of death – the death of buildings and industrial cultures; the death of people, the airmen killed during the war; the death of cars wrecked and burned by joy-riders on Titterstone; and the death of sheep, poor sickly beasts left to fend for themselves, slumping down in illness to die alone on the hillside. One skeleton that I photographed, intact and weathered clean, seemed to have been ignored even by scavenging animals, an image of perfect abandonment [5]. Others I have found half-rotted, trapped in cattle-grids or left out in the open, eyes pecked out, limbs and shredded fleece lying separated from the rest of the body in ghastly images of desolation.

On one summer-evening walk up to the old Abdon Burf quarries with a local historian, we found a pheasant stuck fast, wings flapping, in a tar pool that had been left there when the tarmac plant was dismantled in the 1940s. There was nothing to be done but wring the poor bird's neck. Other hill farmers have tales of larger animals, sheep and even ponies, caught and killed in the tar pools from time to time.

So for all the stillness and silence of the Clee Hills, there is inevitably also a certain menace about them, a threat – something that I thought I saw clearly when I photographed a young sheep, just a few months old, teetering precariously on the steep side of a spoilheap on Clee Burf [4]. Perhaps it is just me, with the sentiments of a townie, but generally the sheep and ponies on the Clee Hills seem always mournful, out in all weathers every month of the year, munching on thin grass between seas of heather and bracken and the scattered detritus of the hills' industrial past [3, 43].

These images of the Clee Hills form a melancholy portfolio, undoubtedly reflecting my own vision of the world and not, by any means, an impartial documentary record of the Clee Hills landscape. There will be many people who love the hills for quite different reasons from those that attract me. For them, my photographs will perhaps strike a false note.

But melancholy is a bittersweet emotion – it is not the same as 'depressing'. In mourning for our losses, for the inexorable passage of time and the brevity of human life, we become more intensely aware of the wonder of human existence and its fragility. I sense melancholy everywhere I walk on the Clee Hills, and that is why I have grown to love them far more intensely than the innumerable prettier places that can be found in the surrounding countryside.

December 2004

3 | Four grazing sheep, Brown Clee

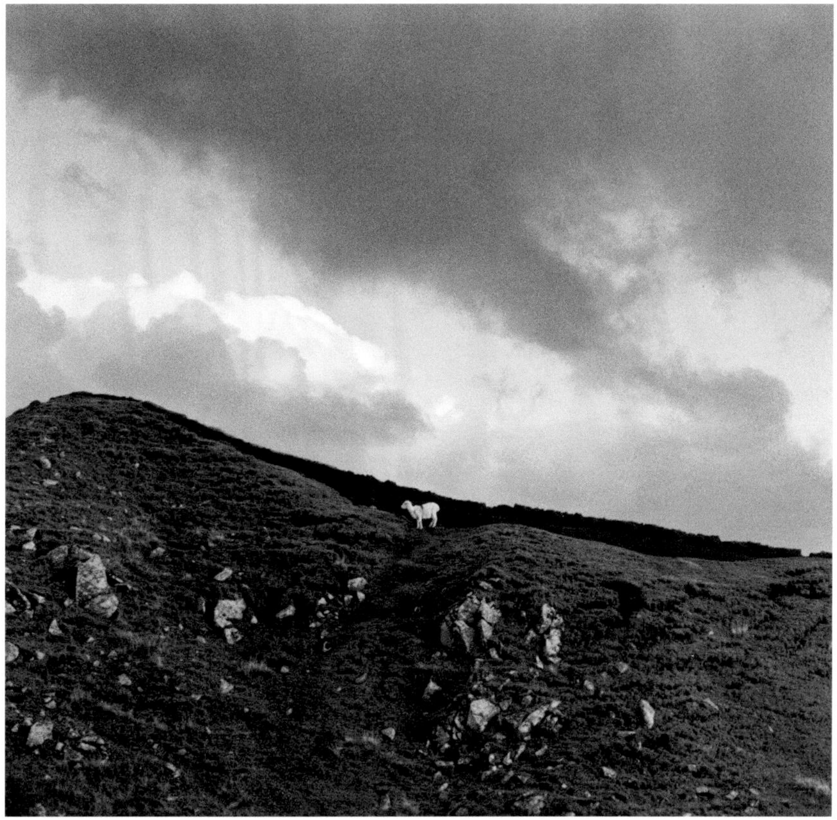

4 | Spoilheap with young sheep, Clee Burf, Brown Clee

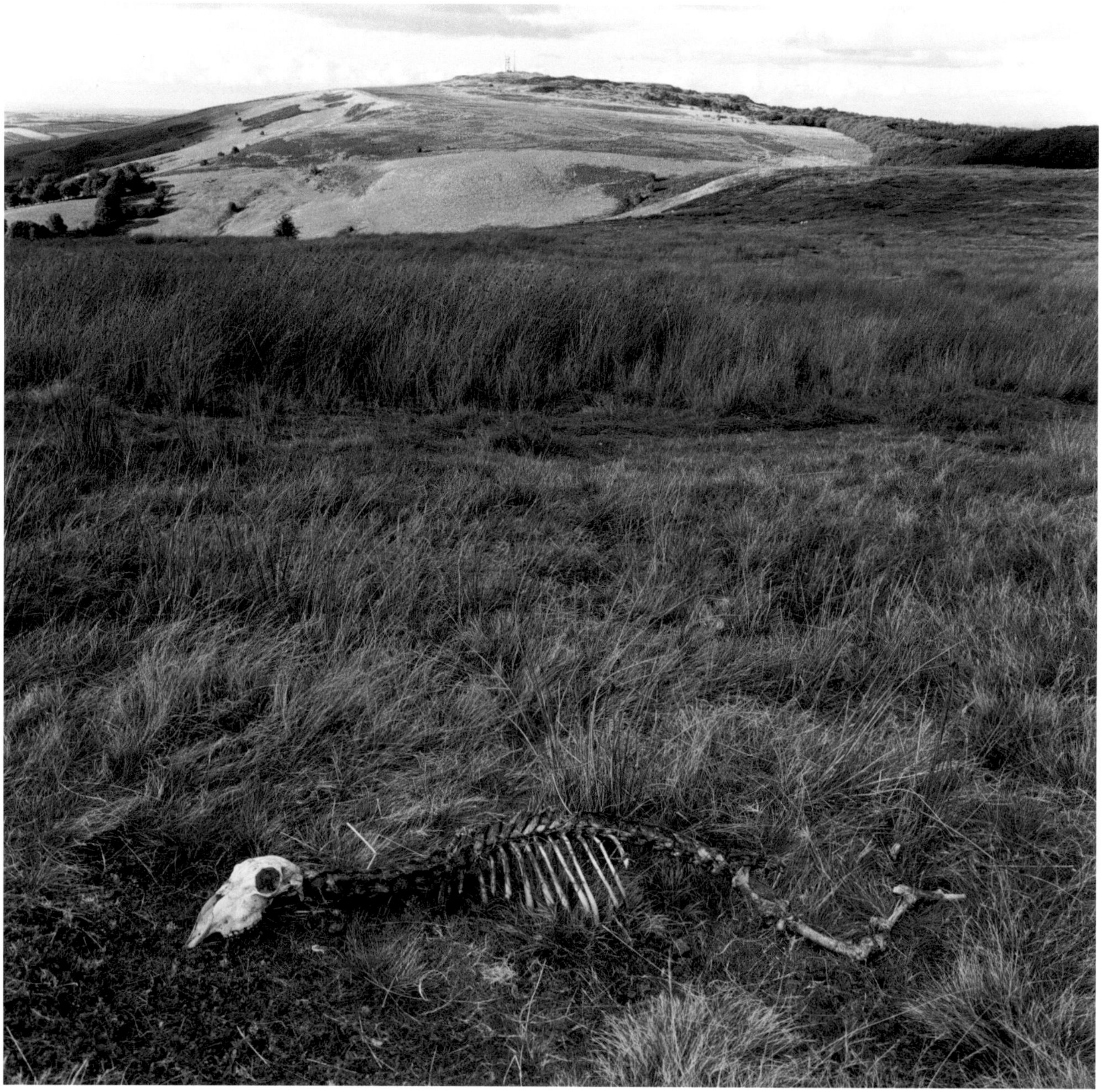

5 | Dead sheep, Brown Clee

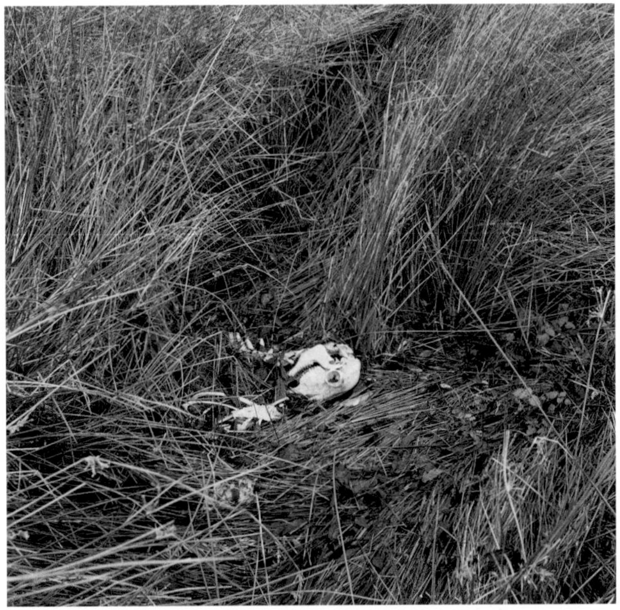

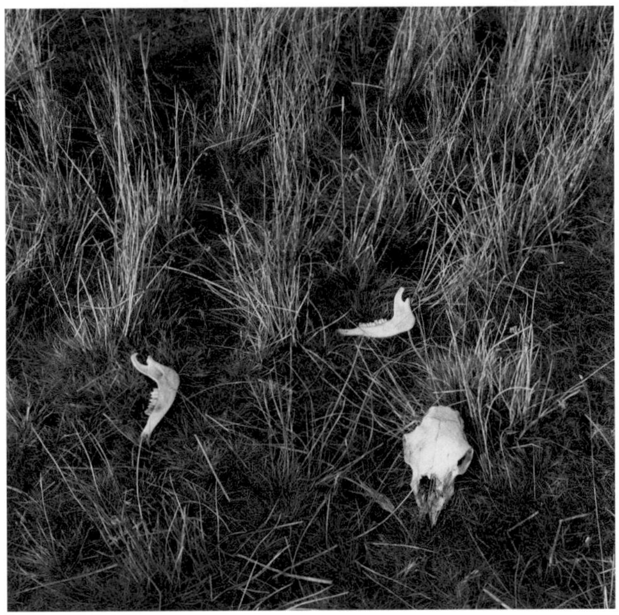

6 | Sheep skull I, Titterstone Clee (top)
7 | Sheep skull II, Brown Clee (bottom)

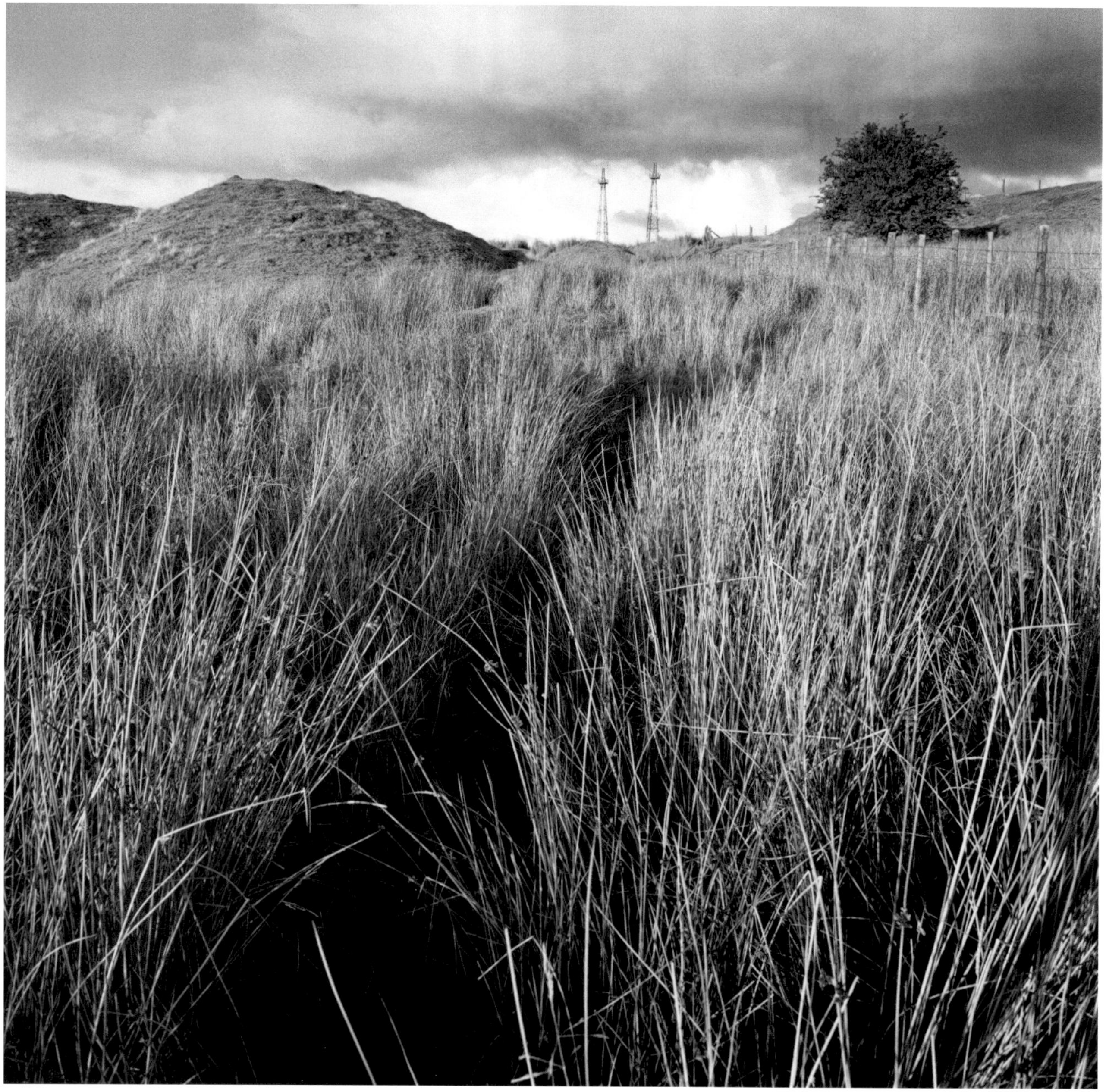

8 | Spoilheaps with radio masts, Clee Burf, Brown Clee

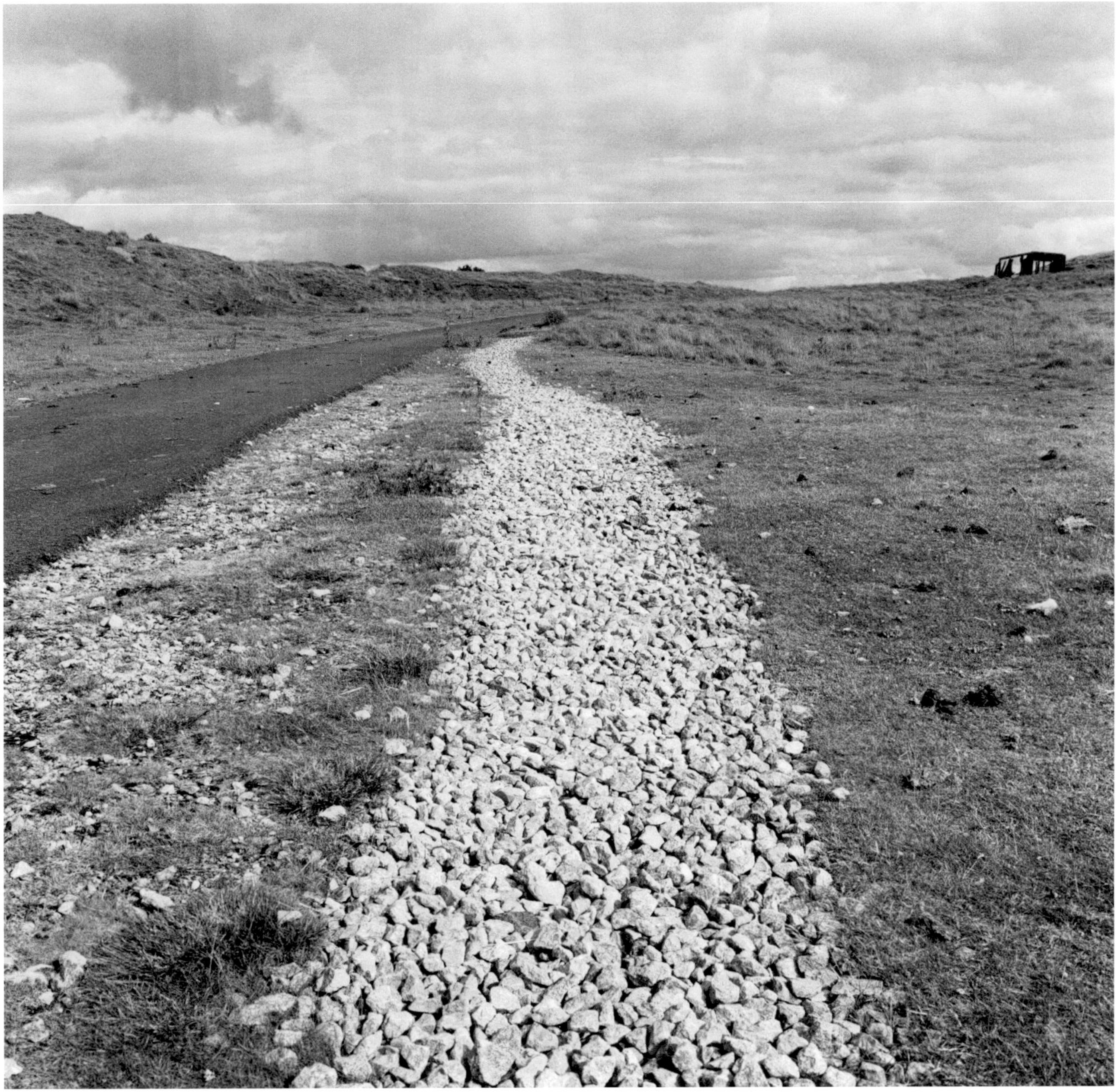

9 | Ruined quarry building with land drain, Abdon Burf, Brown Clee

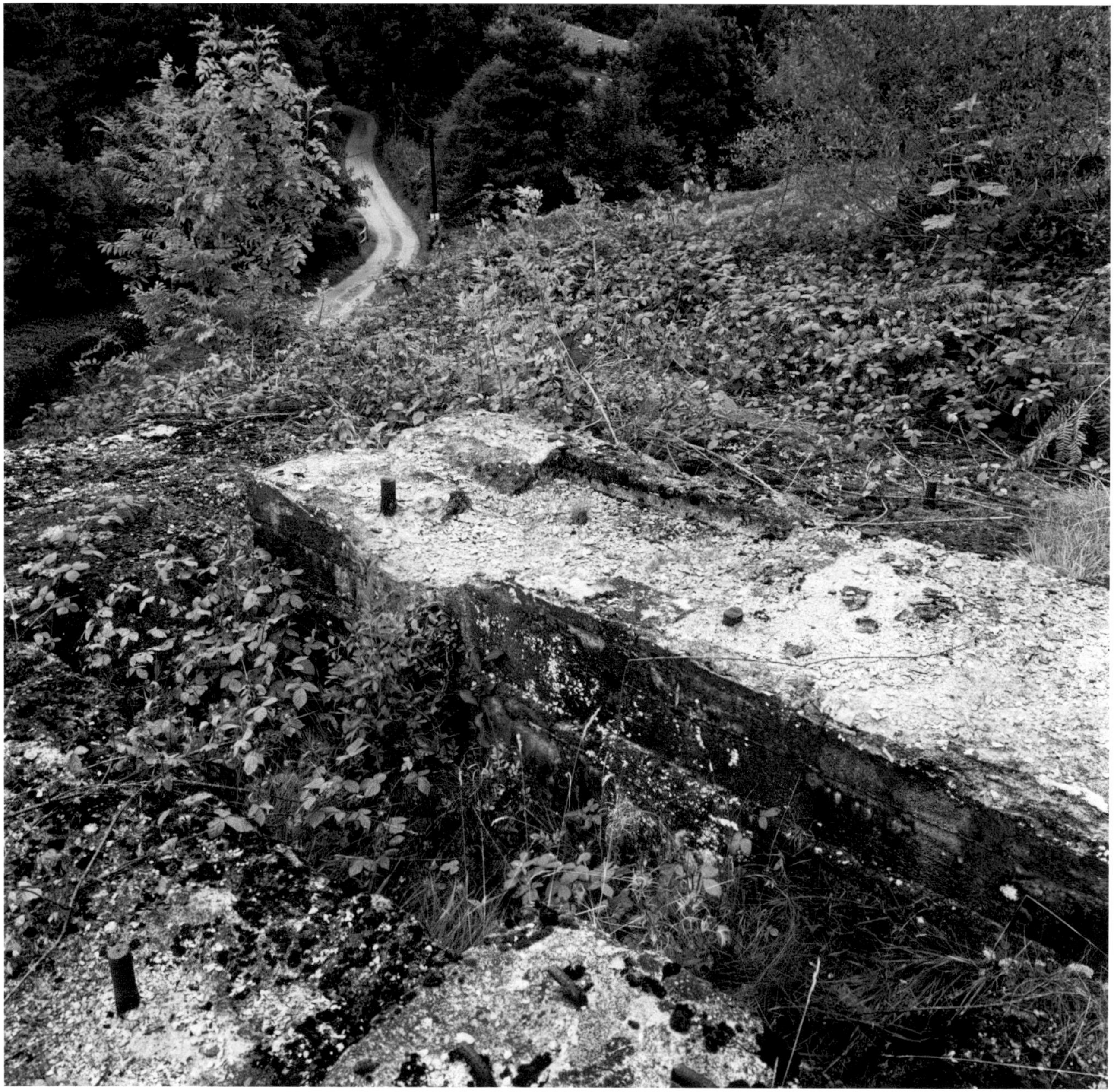

10 | Overgrown lime crusher, Cockshutford, Brown Clee

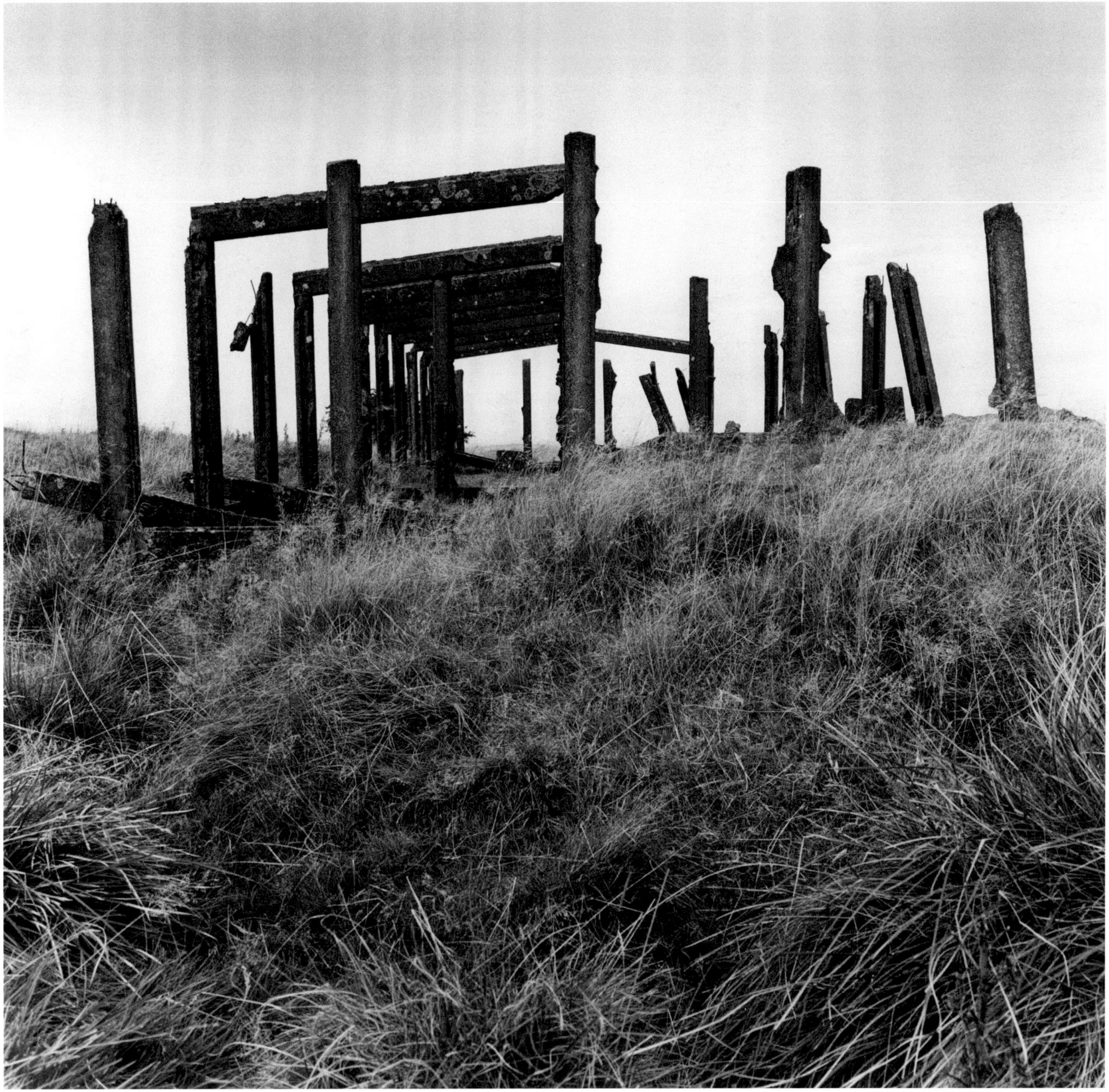

11 | Ruined quarry building, Abdon Burf, Brown Clee*

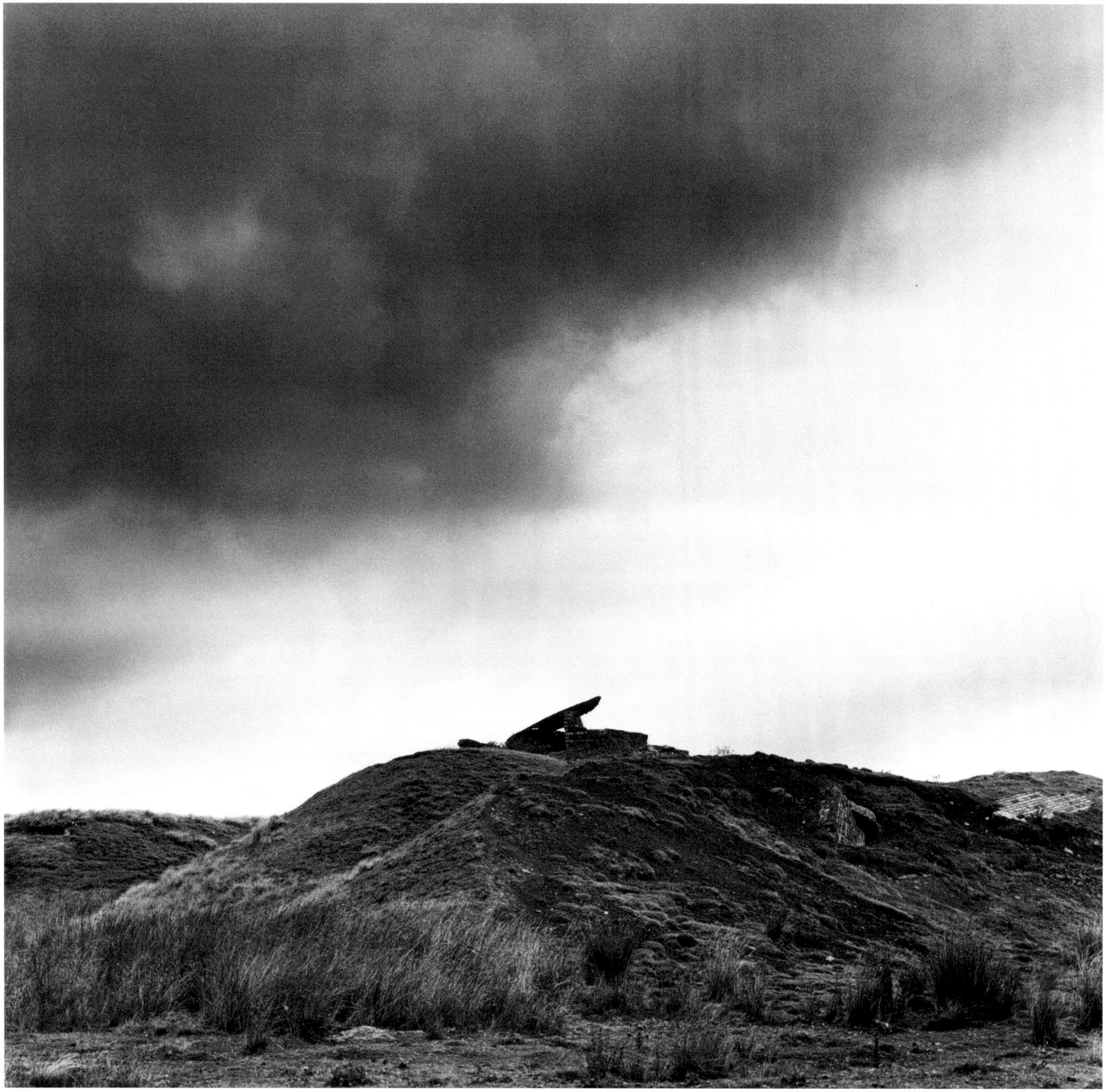

12 | Capped mine shaft, Whatsill, Titterstone Clee

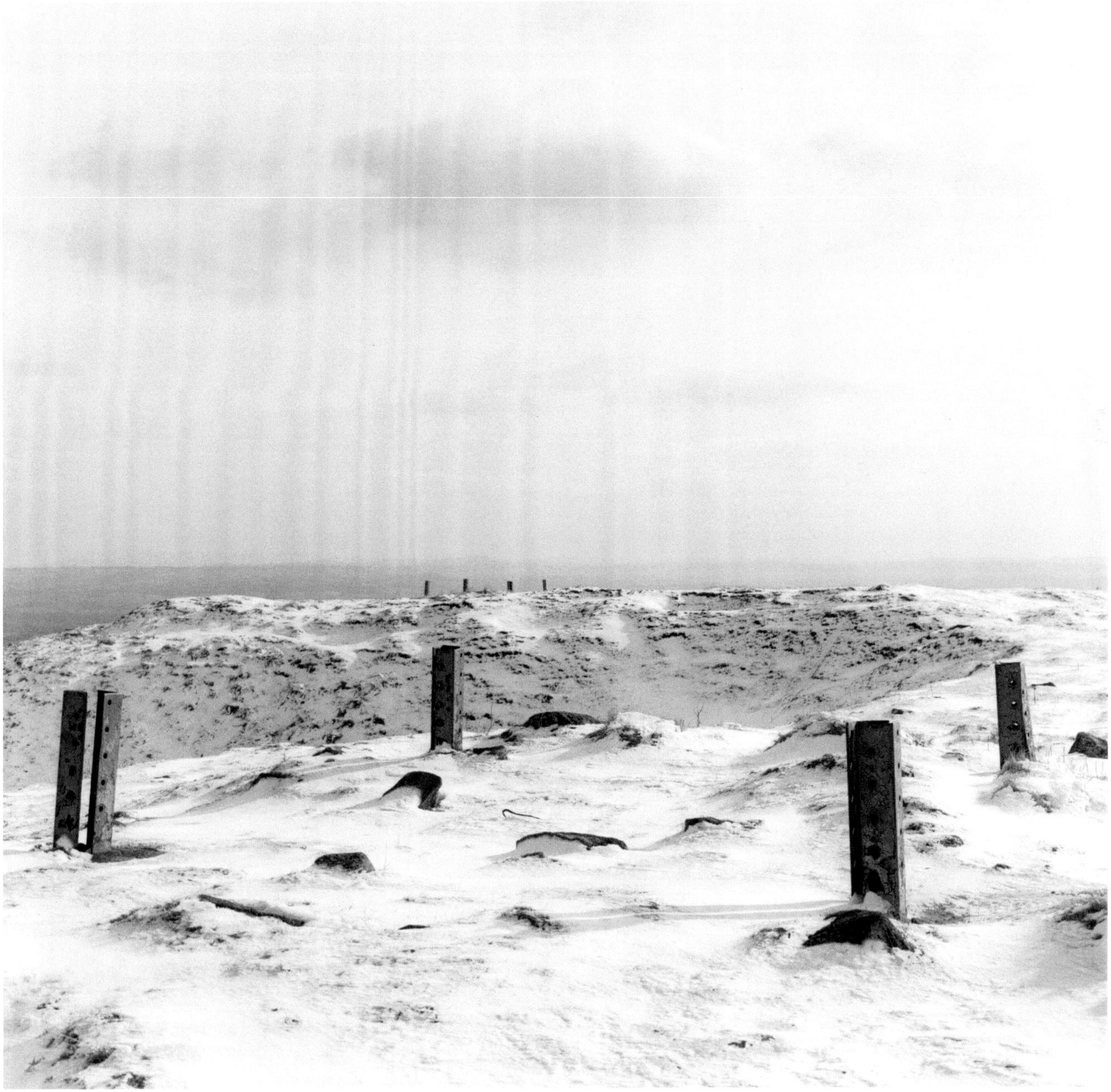

13 | Pylon footings, Whatsill, Titterstone Clee

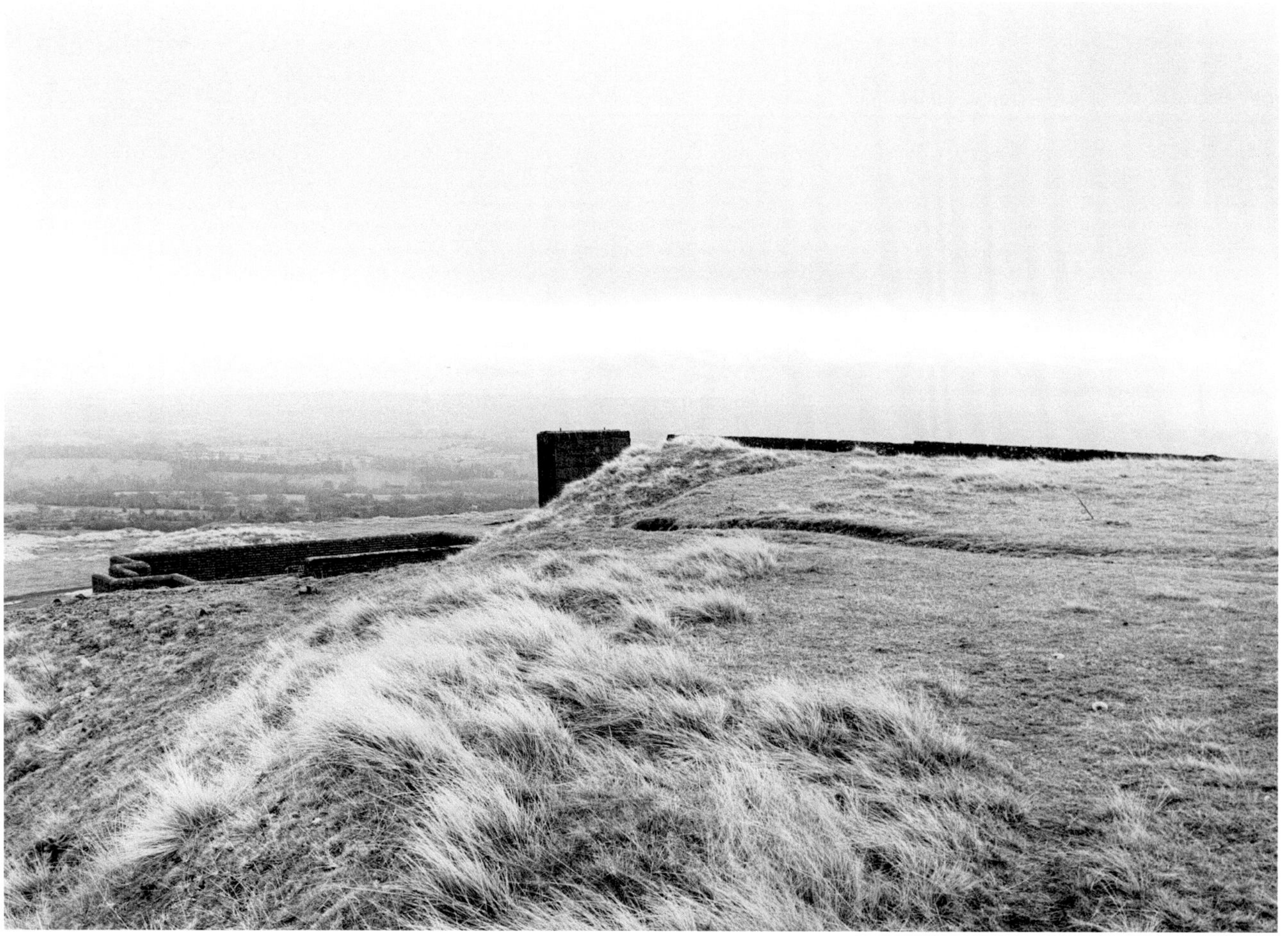

14 | Crusher buildings, Magpie Hill, Titterstone Clee

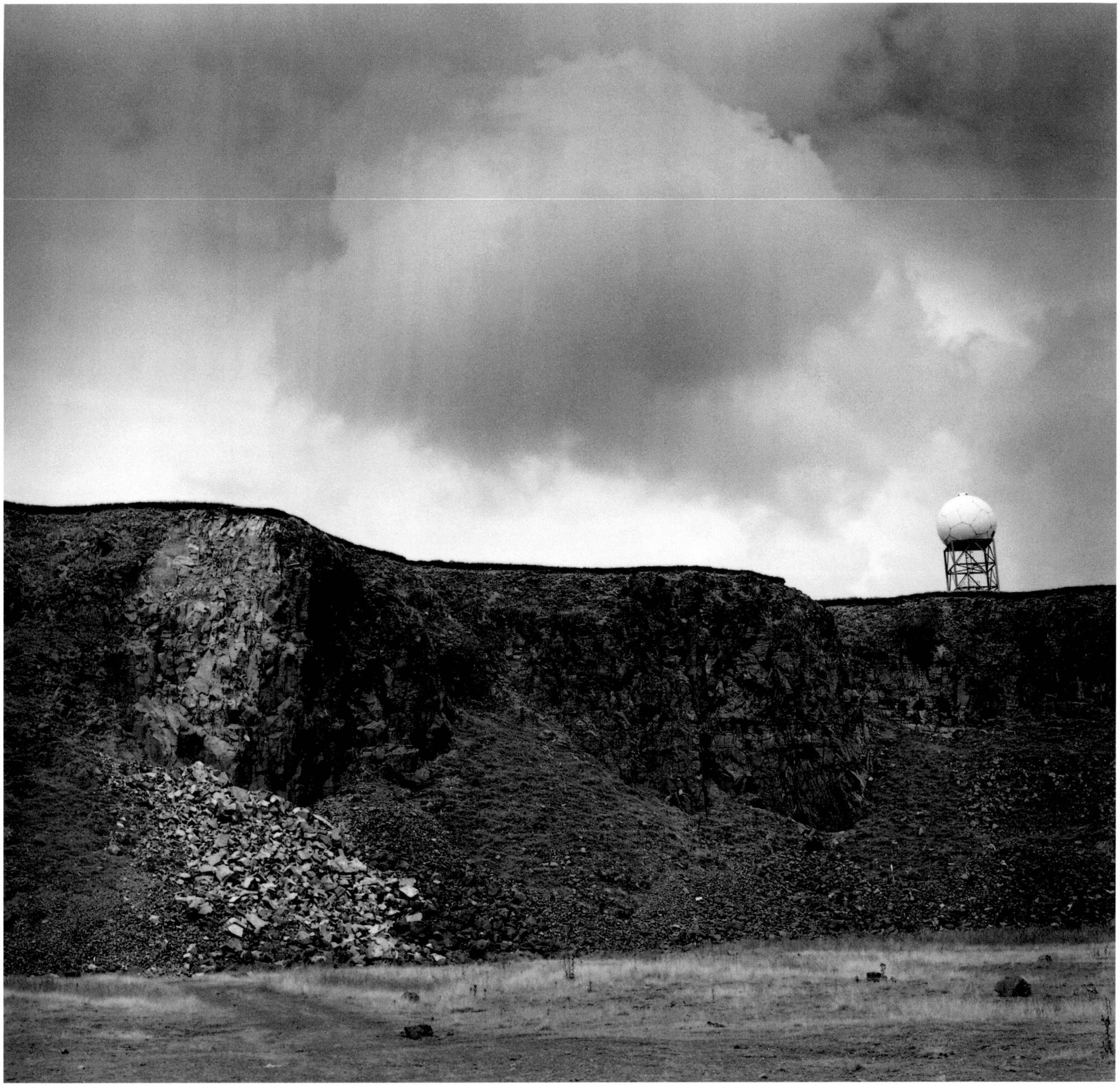

15 | Abandoned quarry, Titterstone Clee*

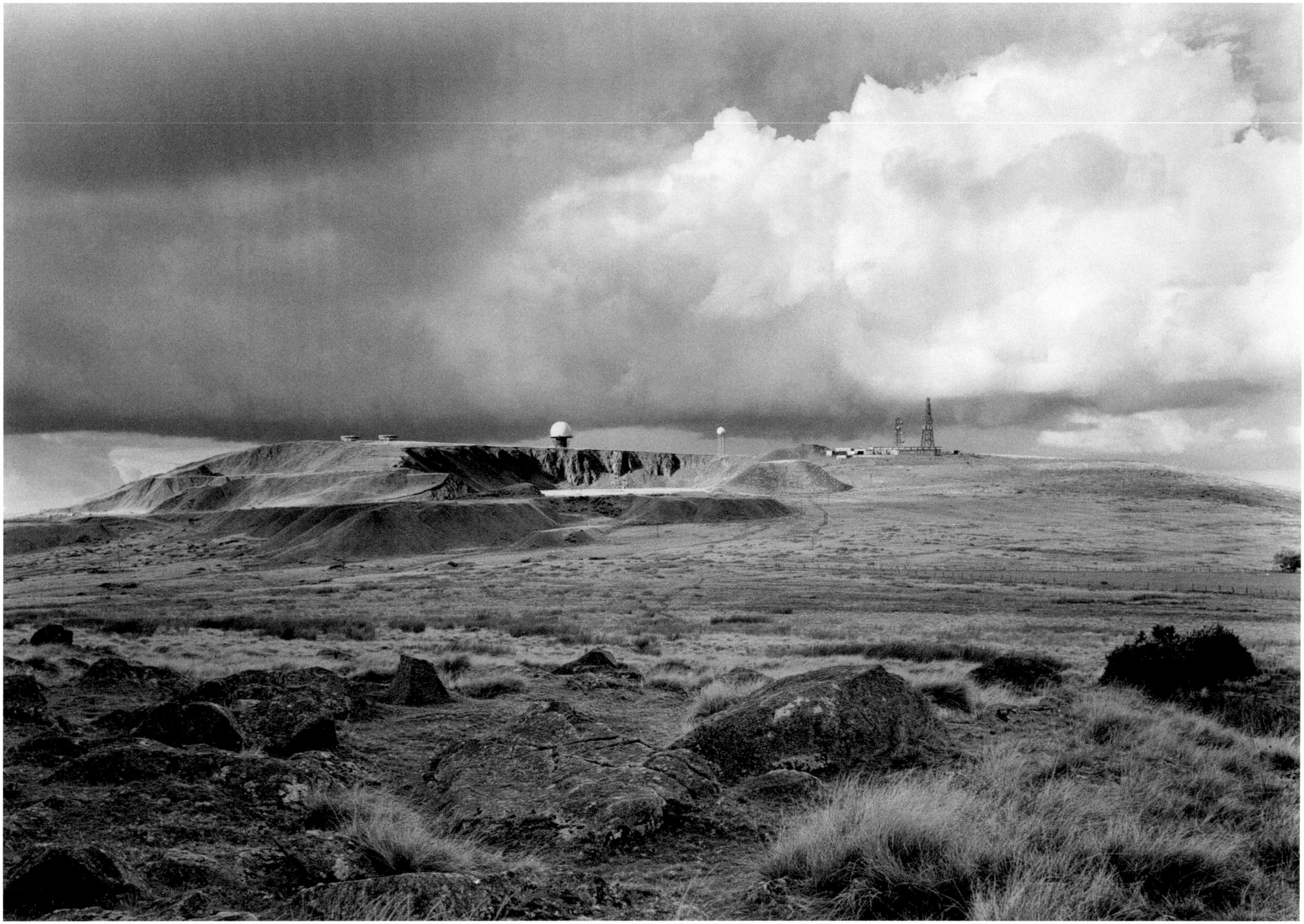

16 | Abandoned quarries with radar station, Titterstone Clee summit

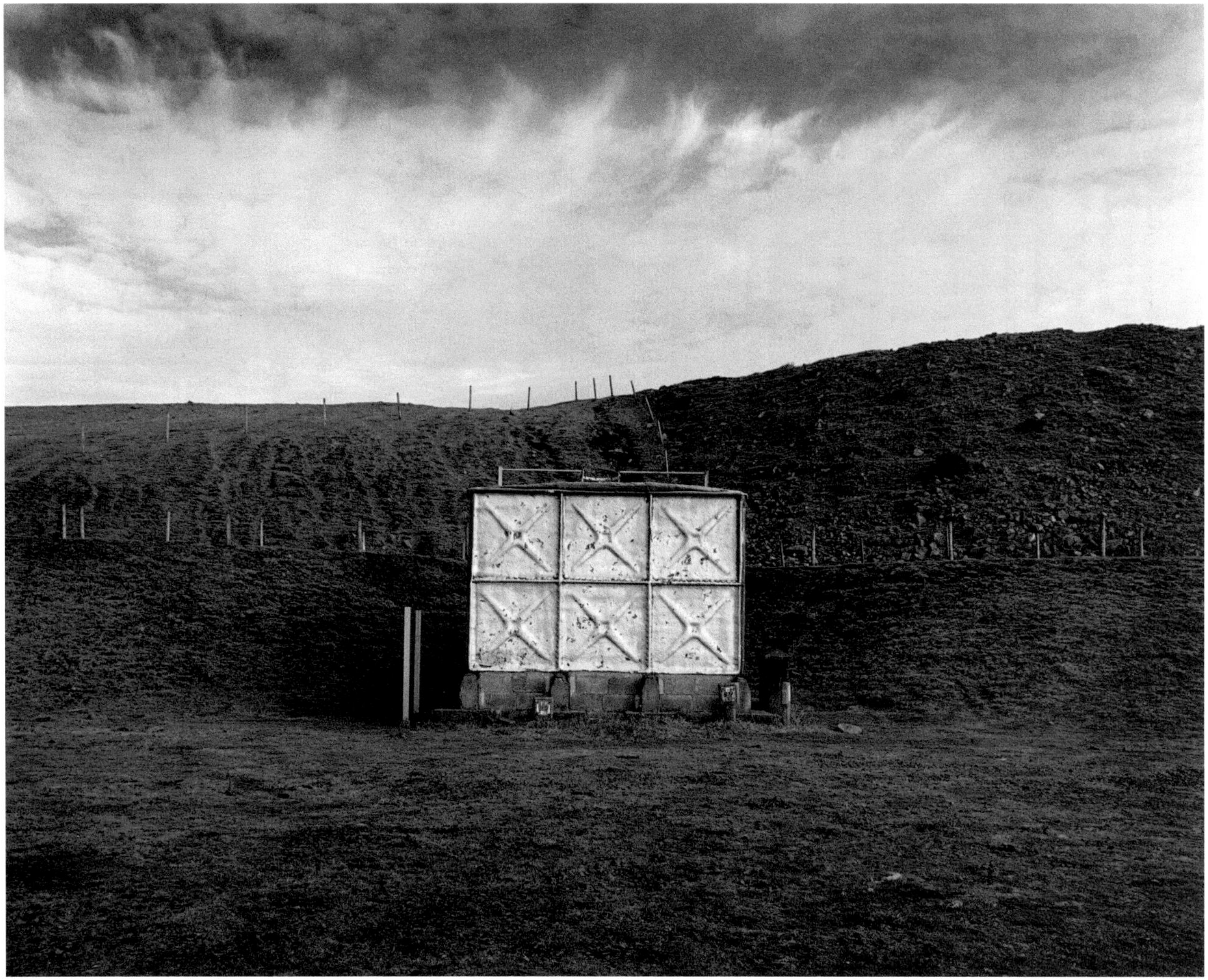

17 | Watertank, Dhustone, Titterstone Clee*

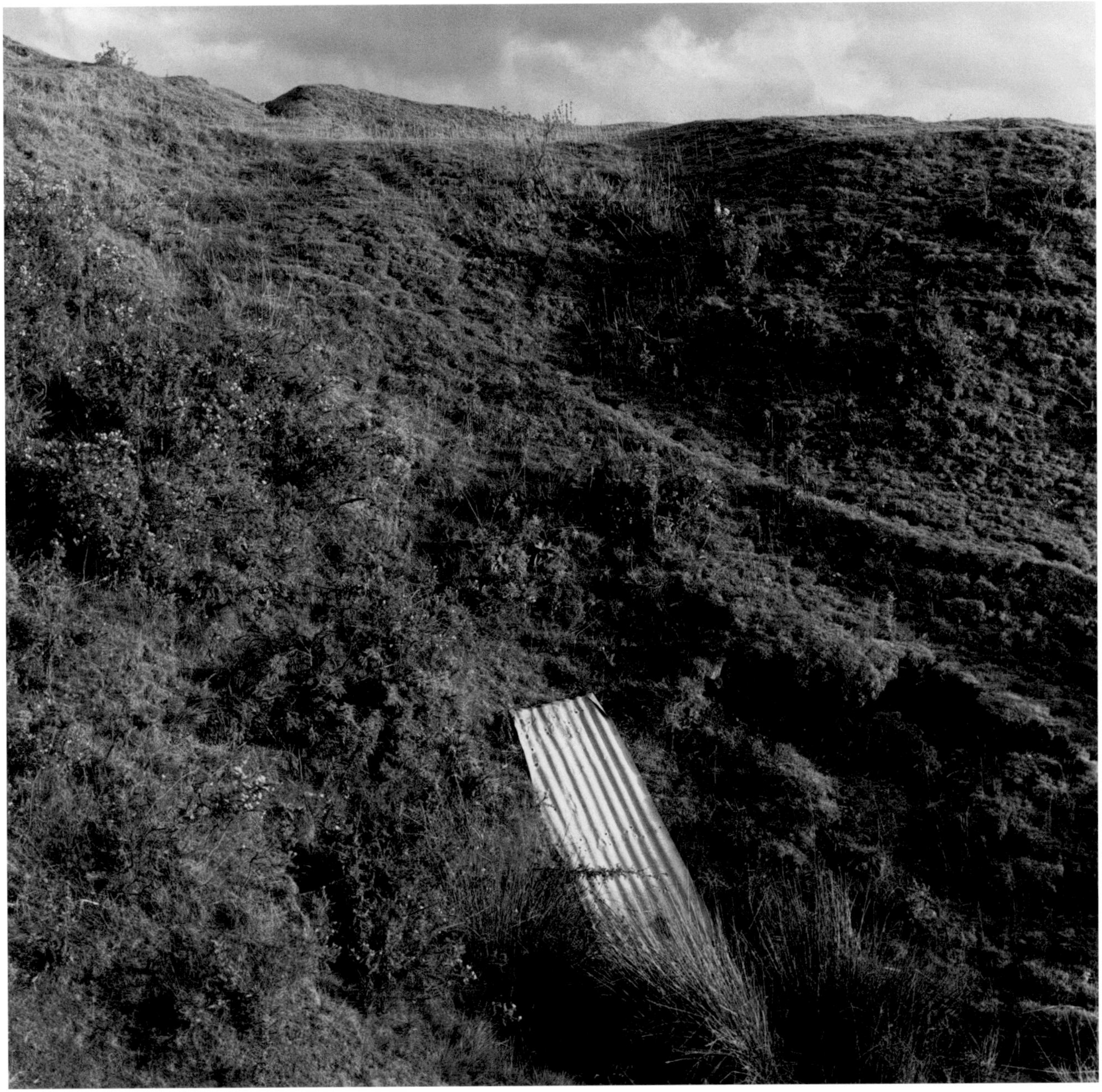

18 | Spoilheaps with corrugated iron sheet, Titterstone Clee

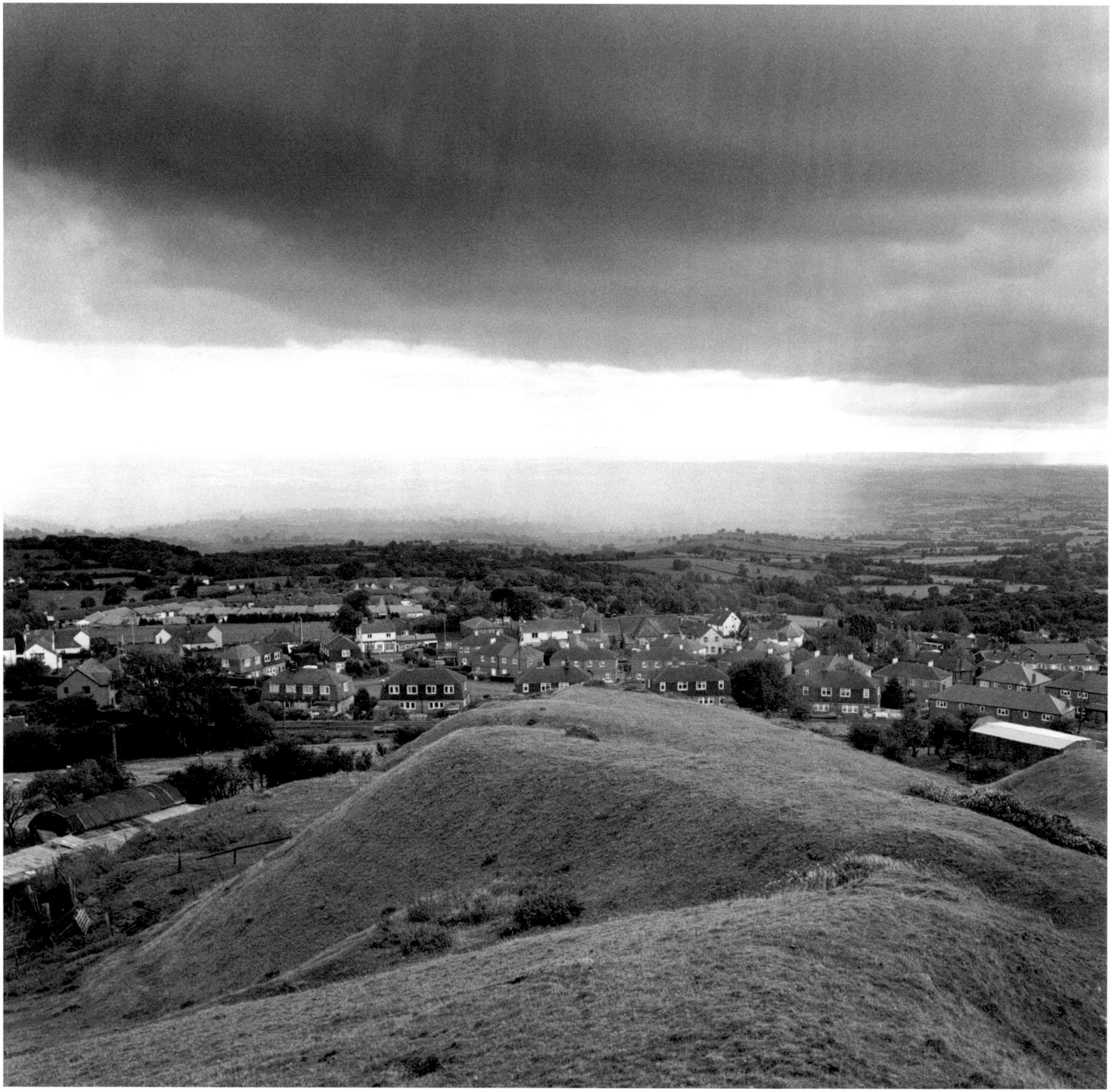

19 | Spoilheaps over Clee Hill village, Titterstone Clee

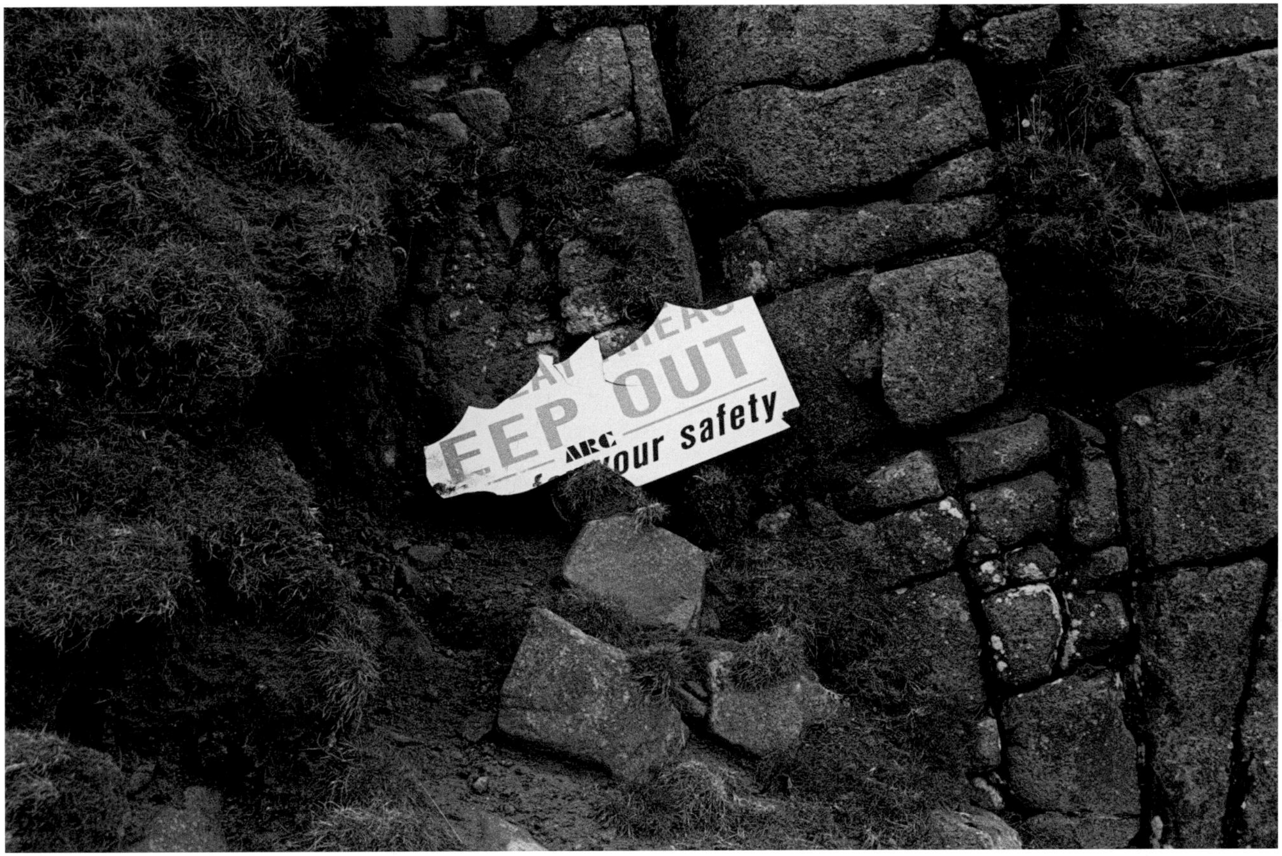

20 | 'Keep Out' I, Titterstone Clee

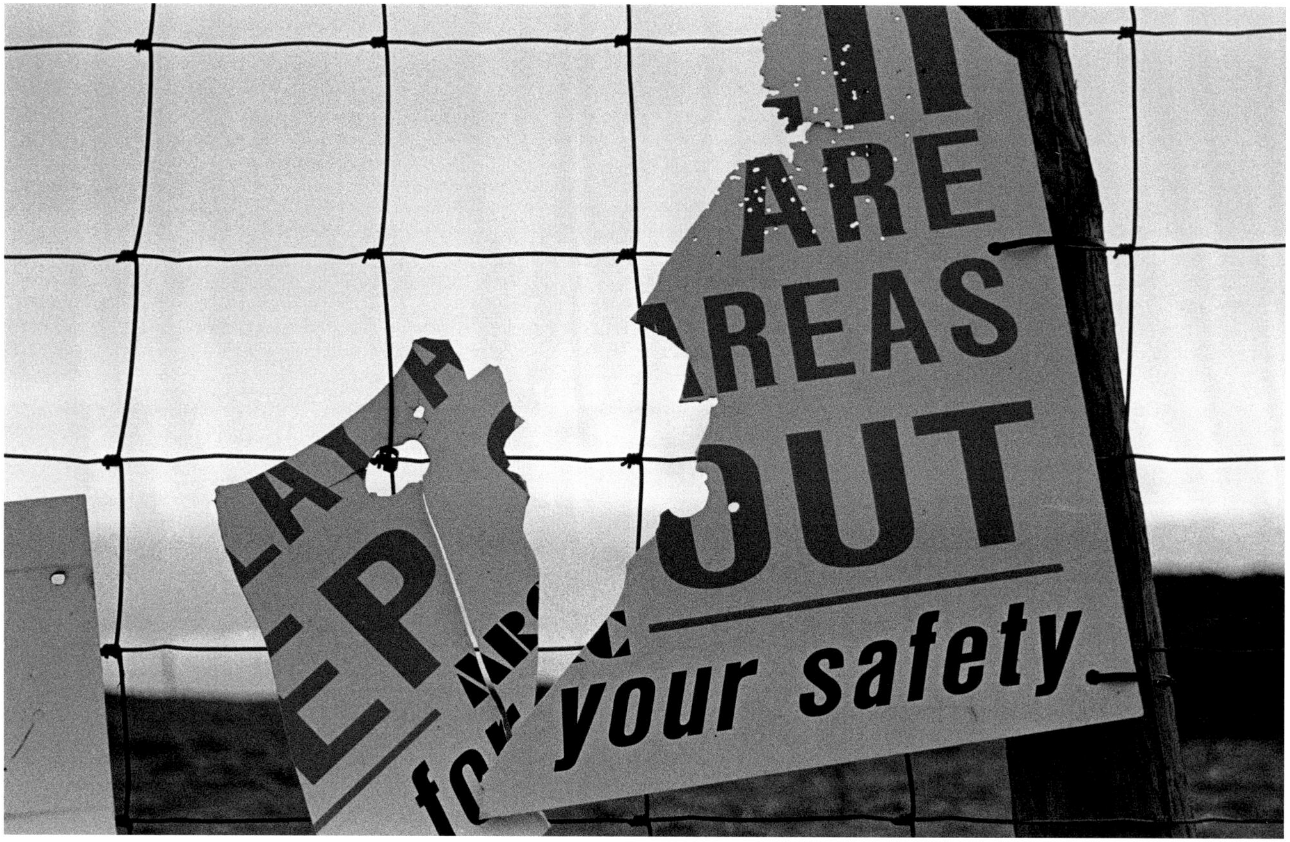

21 | 'Keep Out' II, Titterstone Clee

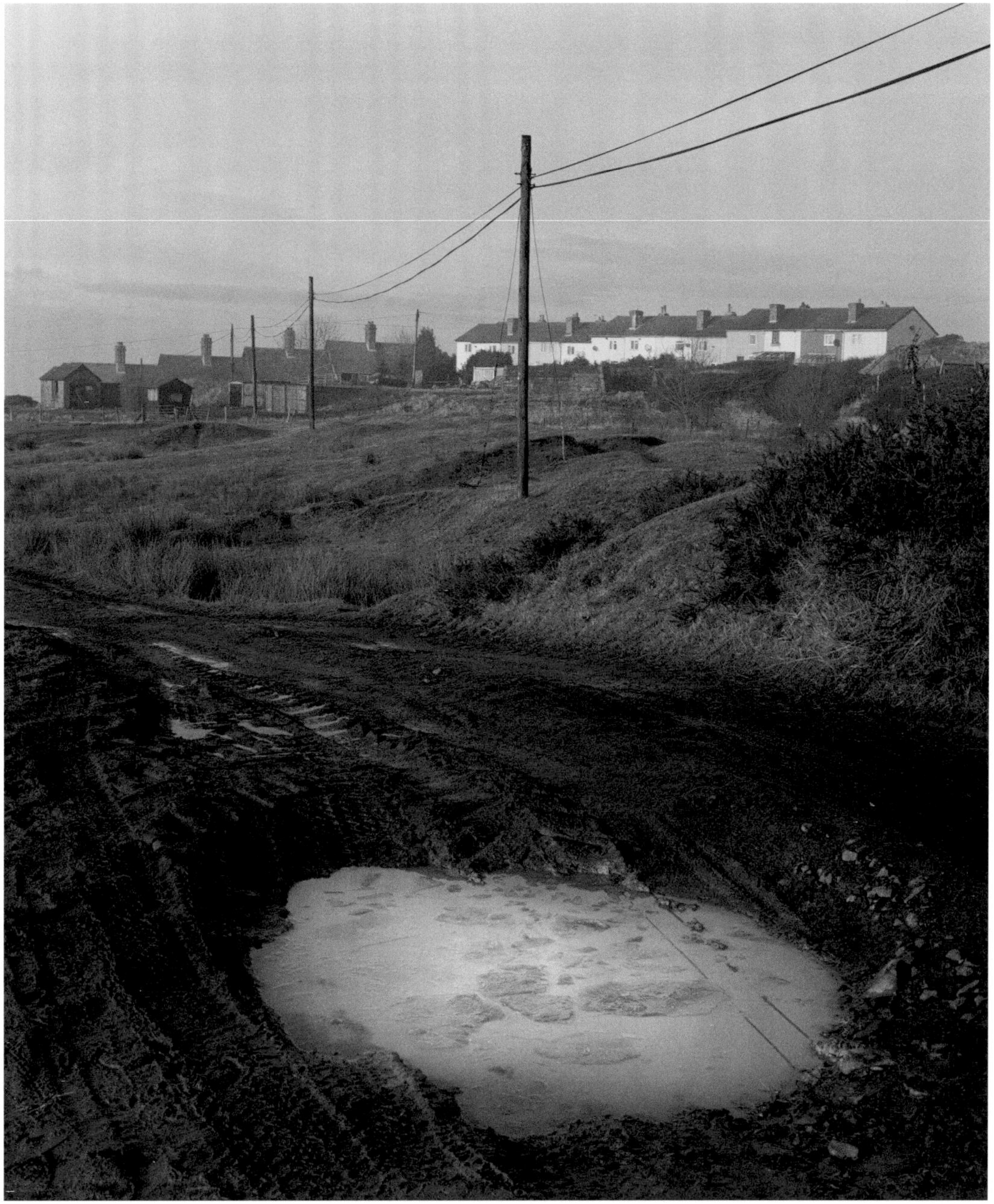

22 | Quarry workers' housing, Dhustone, Titterstone Clee

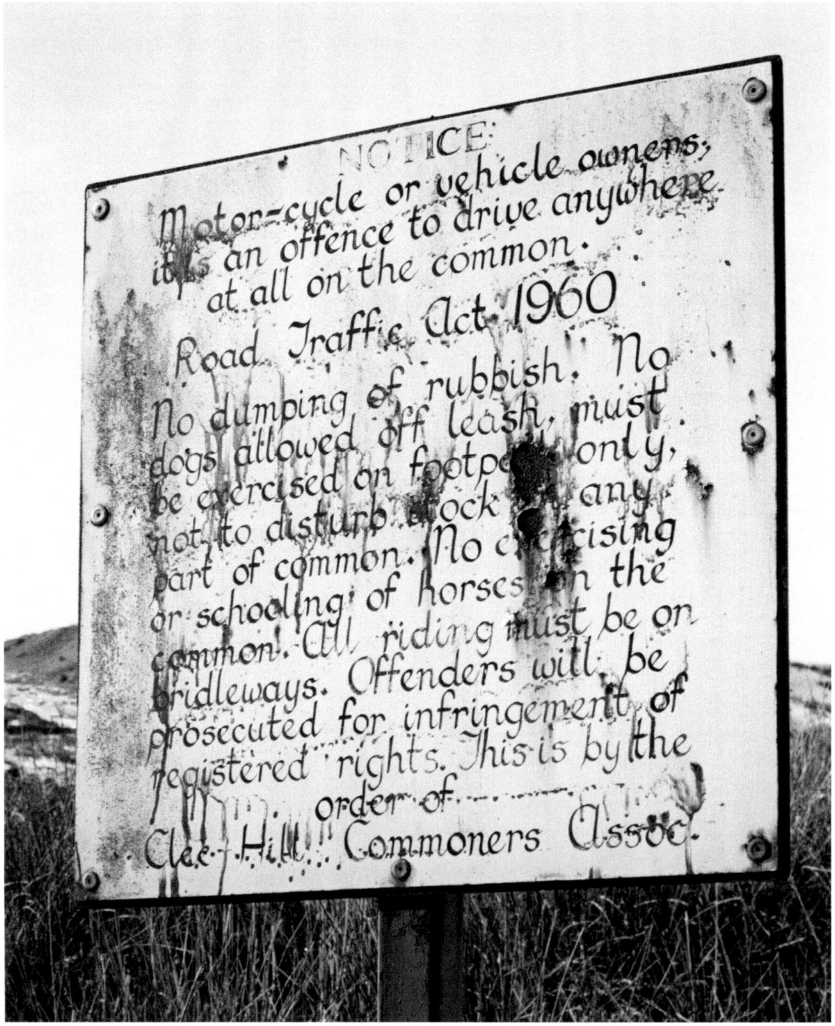

23 | Stained notice, Doddington, Titterstone Clee

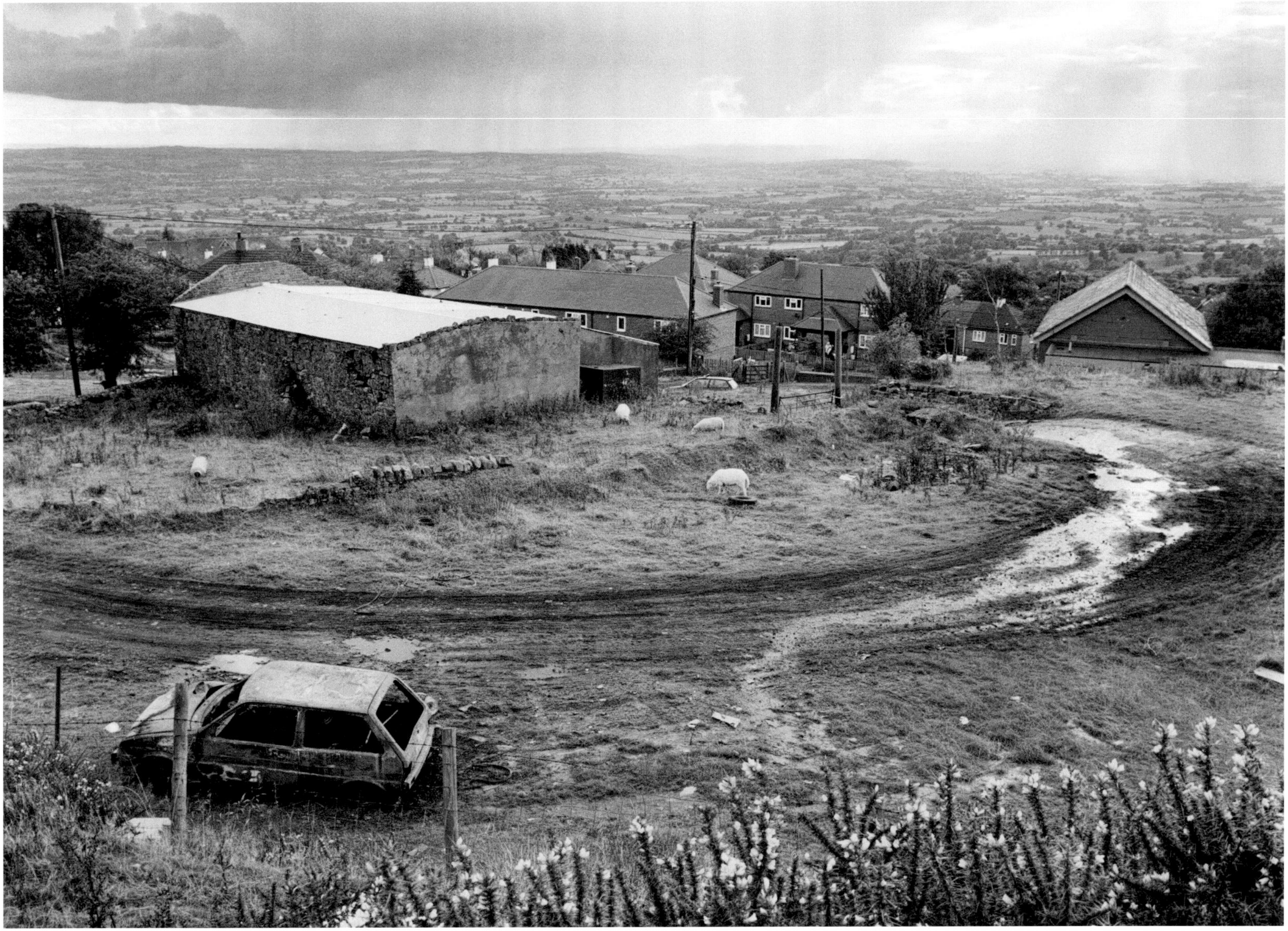

24 | Burnt-out car with water trail, Clee Hill village, Titterstone Clee

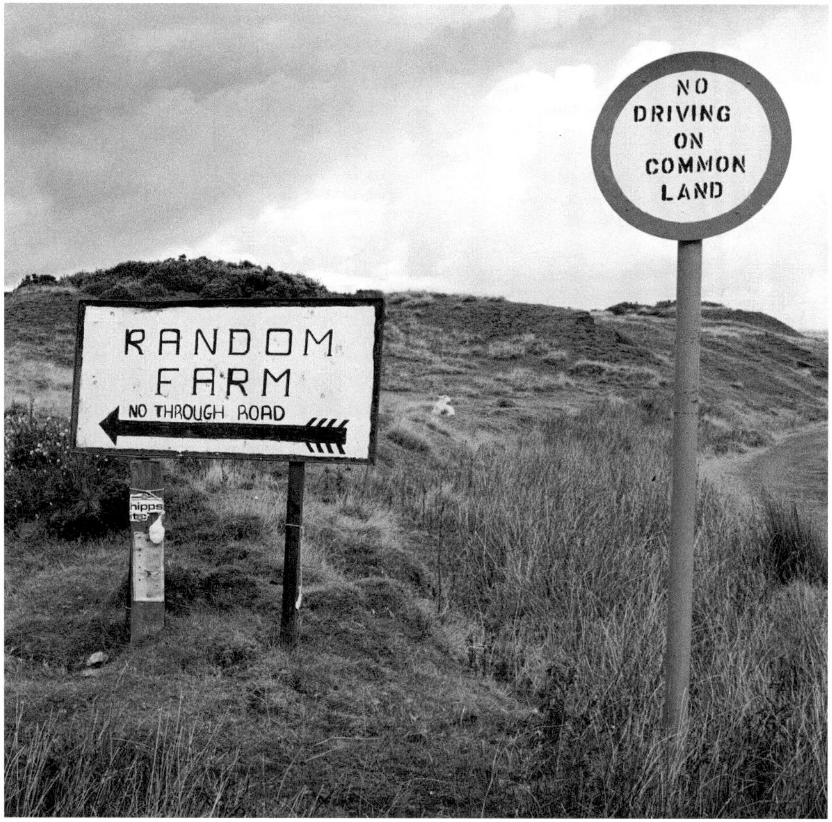

25 | 'No Driving on Common Land', Random, Titterstone Clee

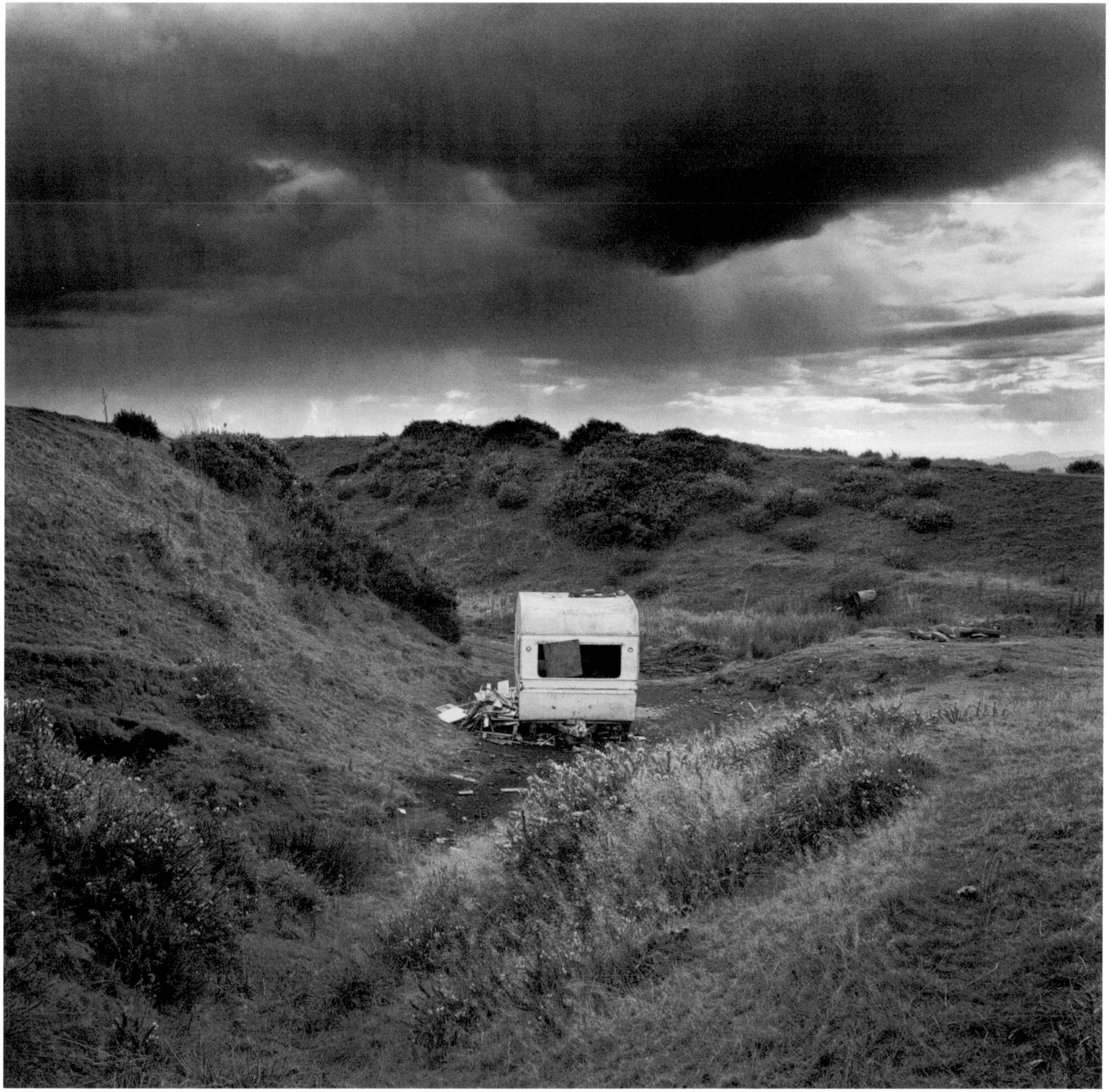

26 | Dumped caravan, Titterstone Clee

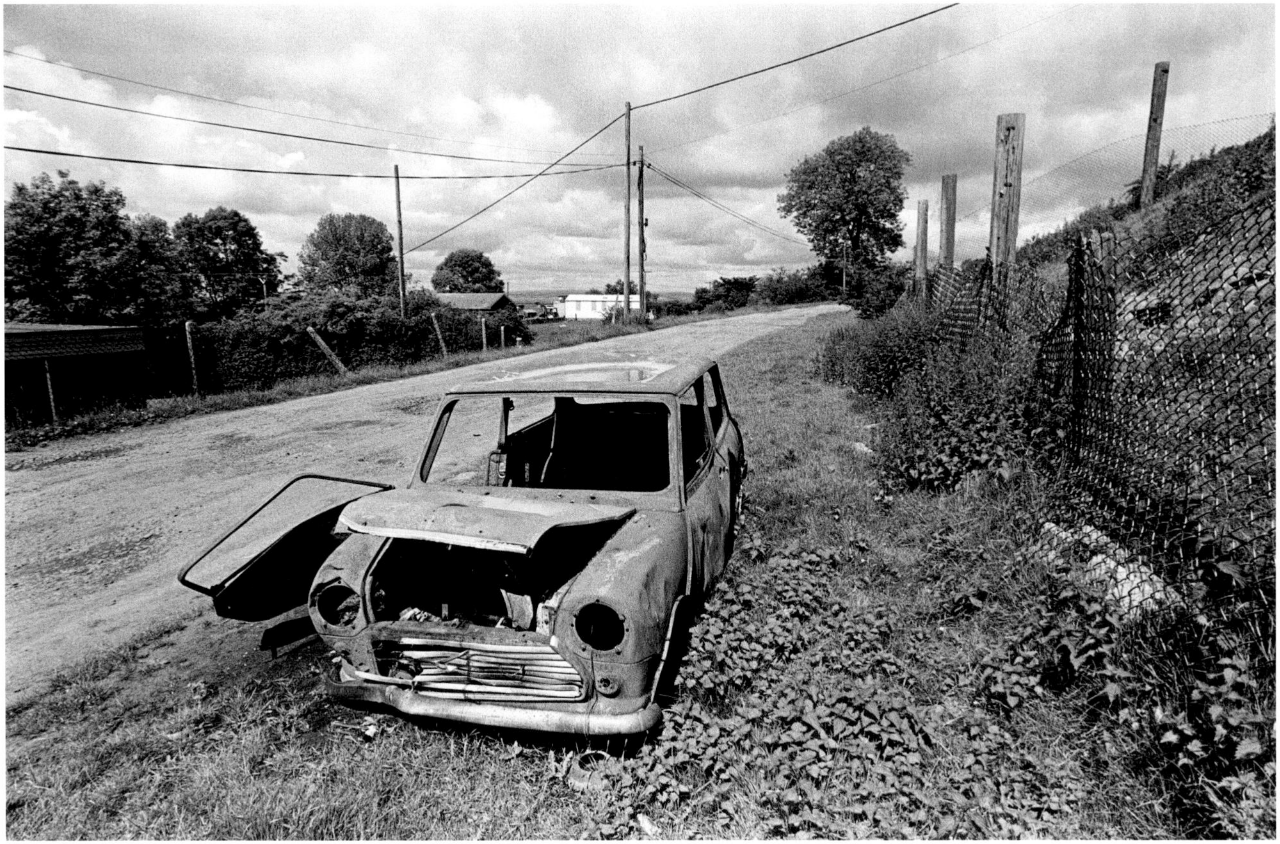

27 | Burnt-out car by former railway line, Clee Hill village, Titterstone Clee

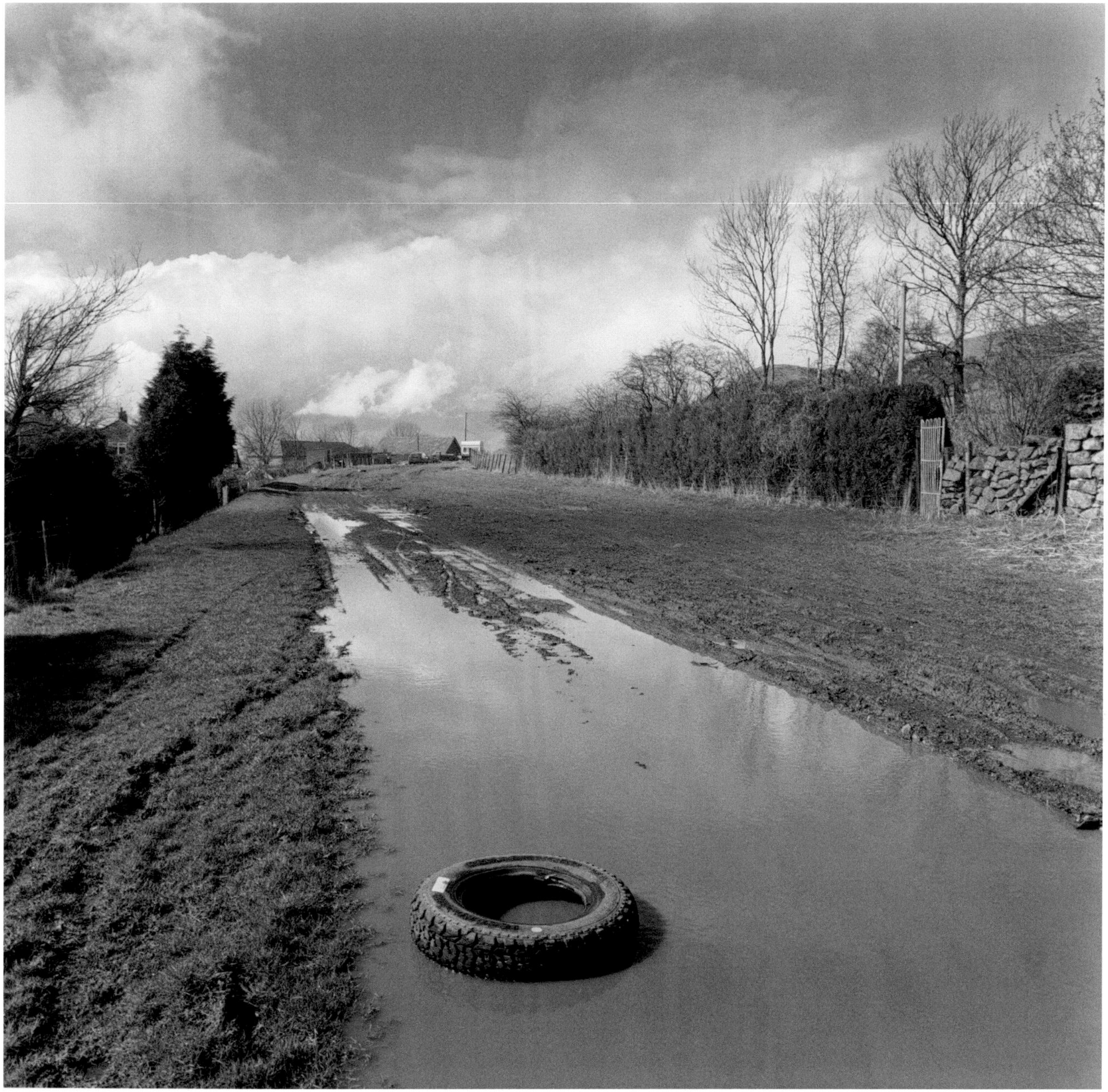

28 | Disused railway line with car tyre, Clee Hill village, Titterstone Clee

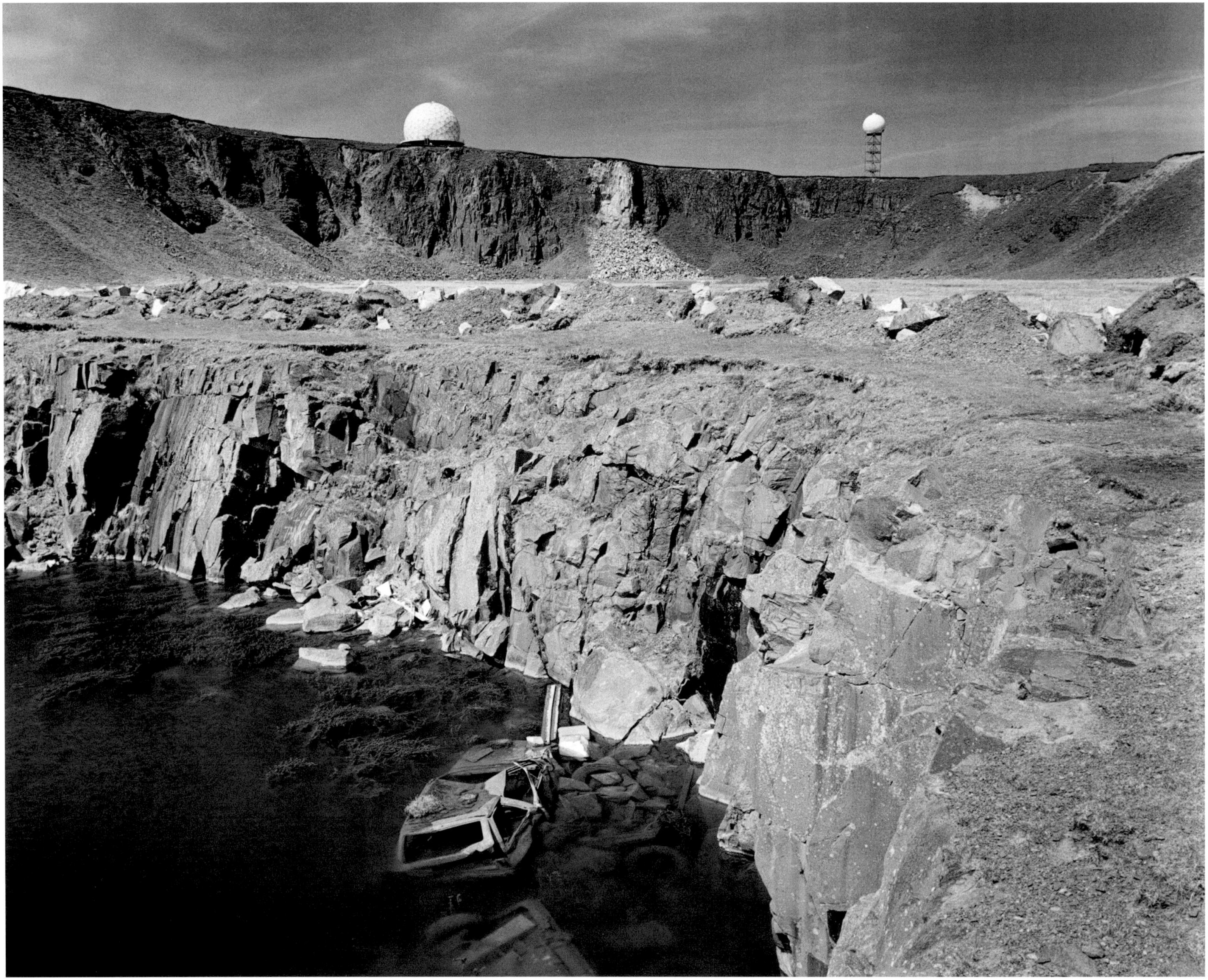

29 | Abandoned quarry with two drowned cars, Titterstone Clee

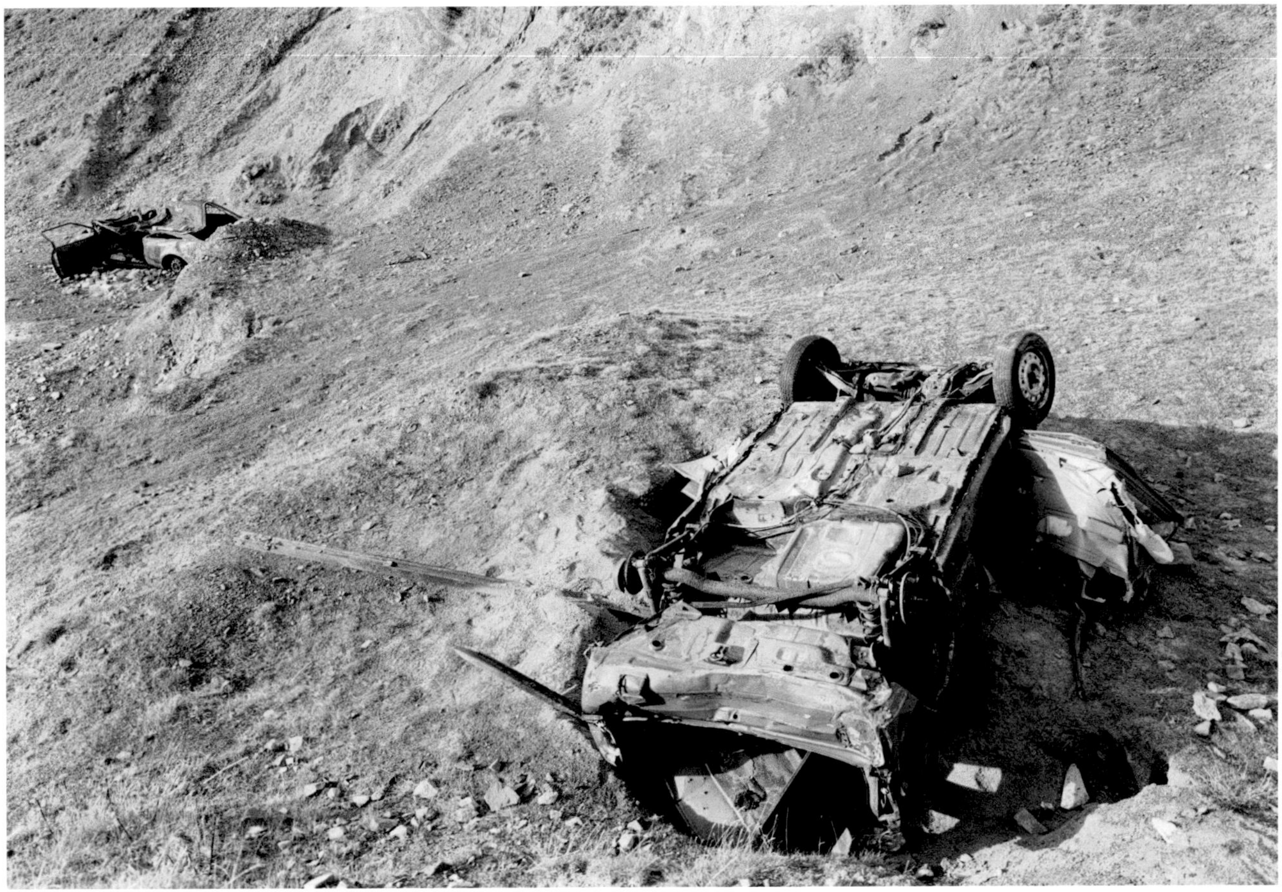

30 | Wrecked cars, Titterstone Clee

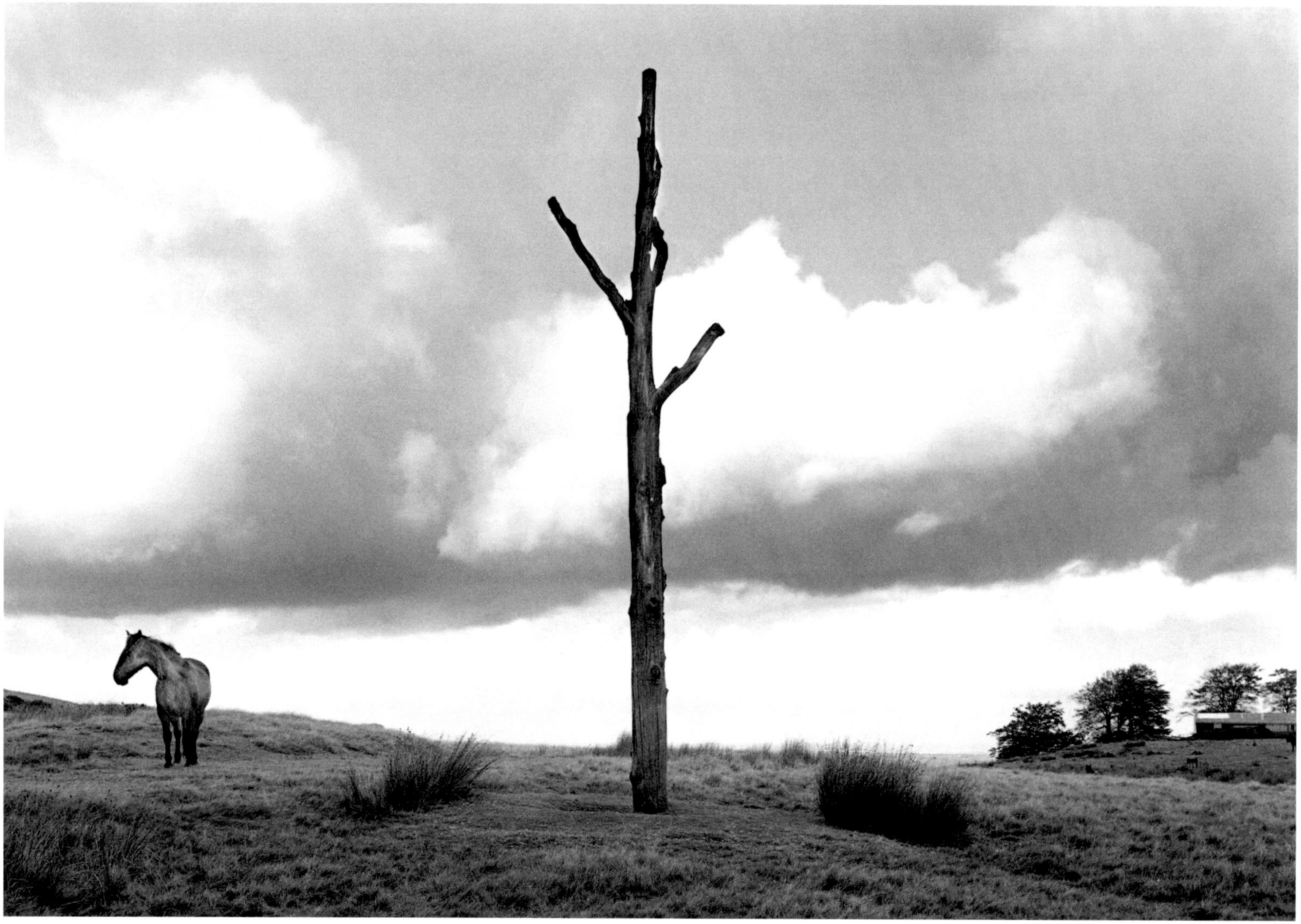

31 | Tree-post and horse (the 'Three-Forked Pole'), Random, Titterstone Clee*

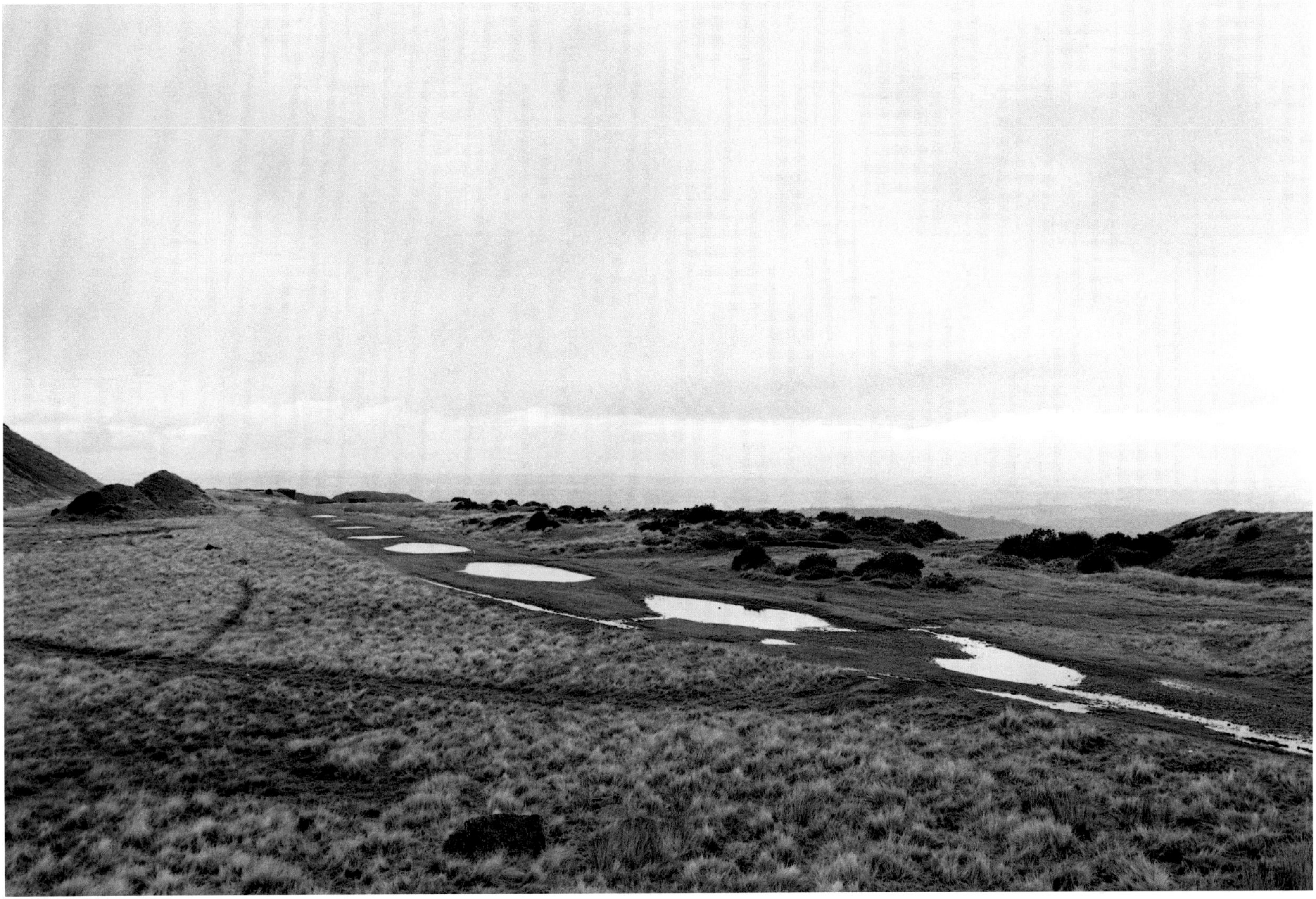

32 | Former quarry road, Magpie Hill, Titterstone Clee*

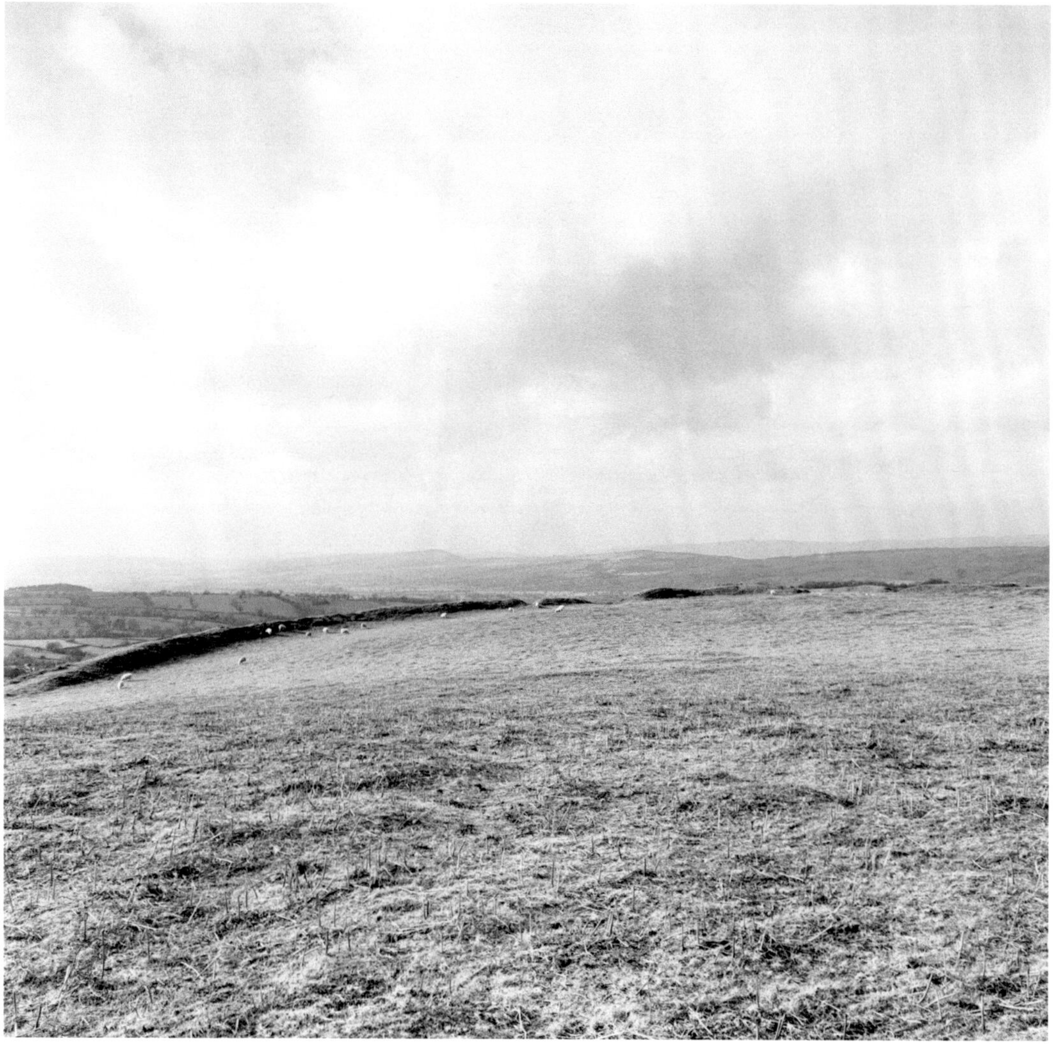

33 | Nordy Bank hillfort, Brown Clee

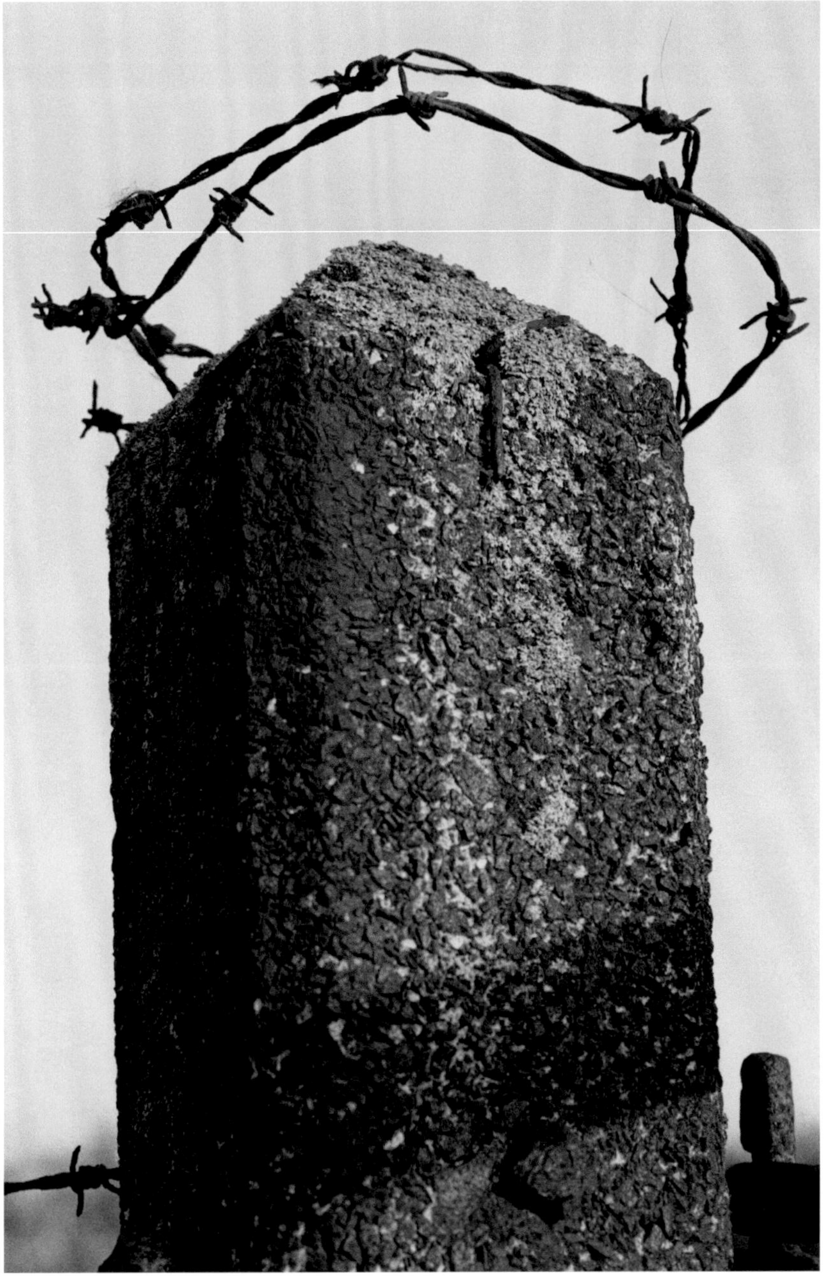

34 | Gatepost with barbed wire, Brown Clee

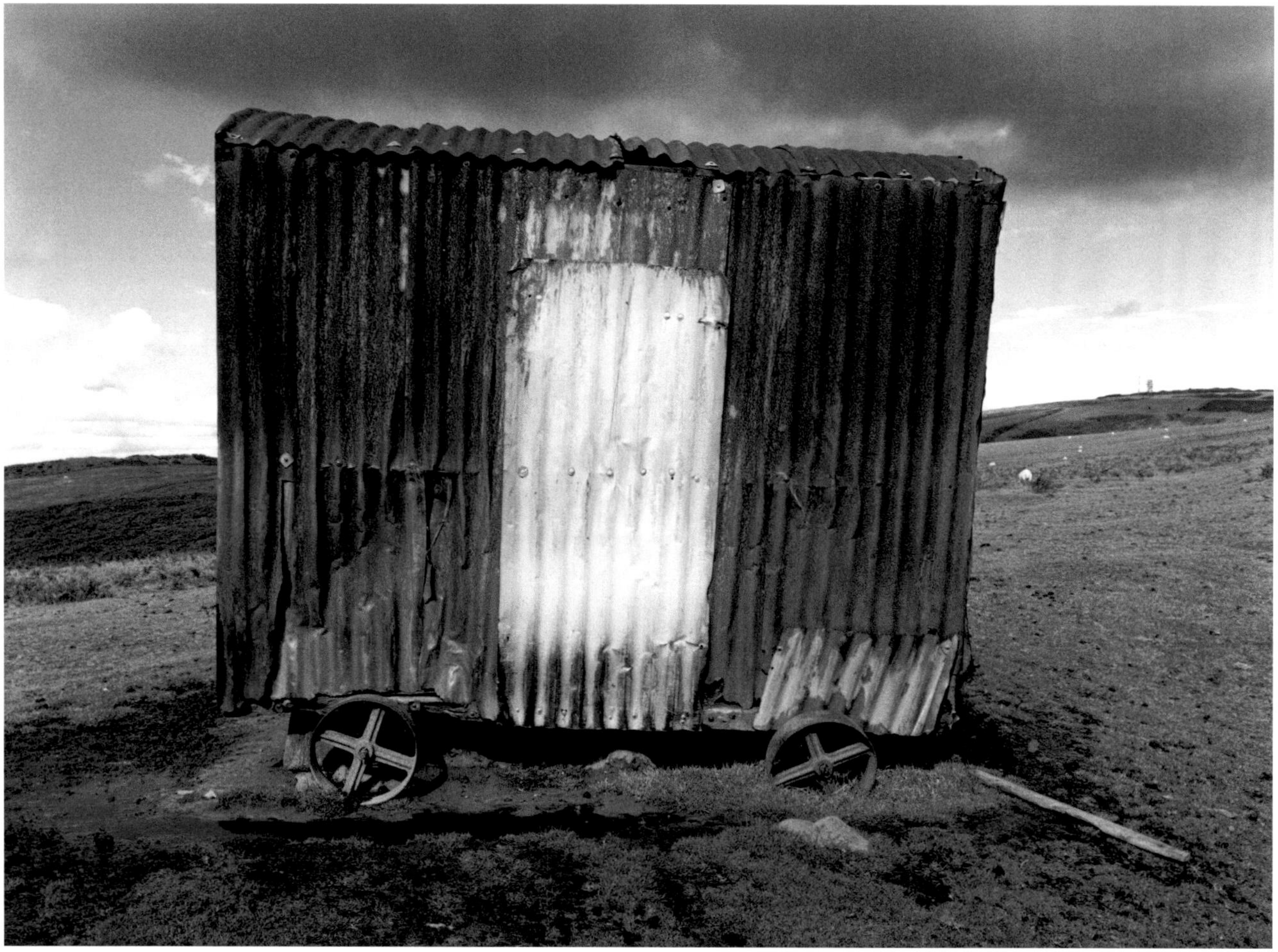

35 | Sheep shed, Brown Clee*

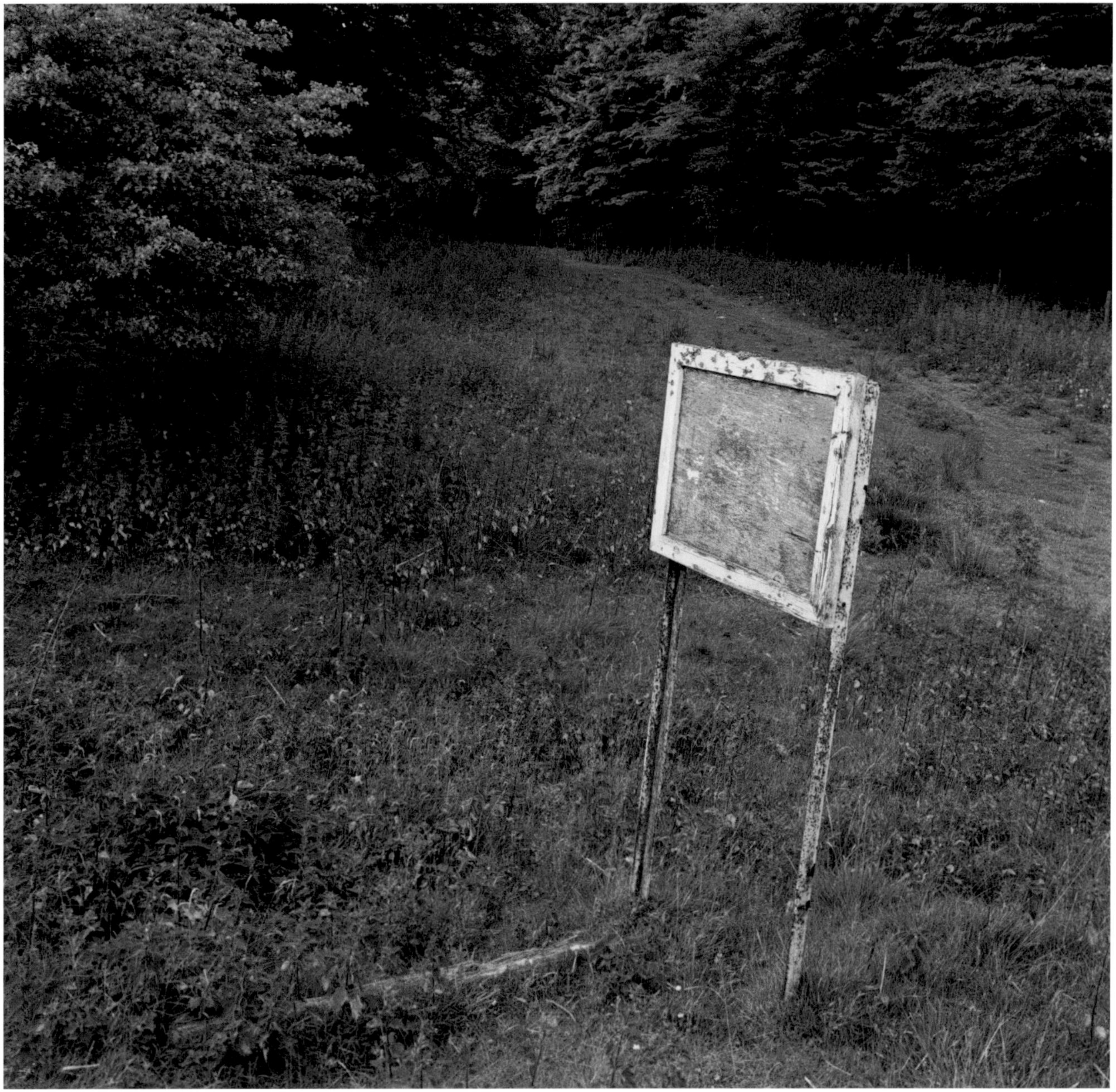

36 | White signpost, Brown Clee

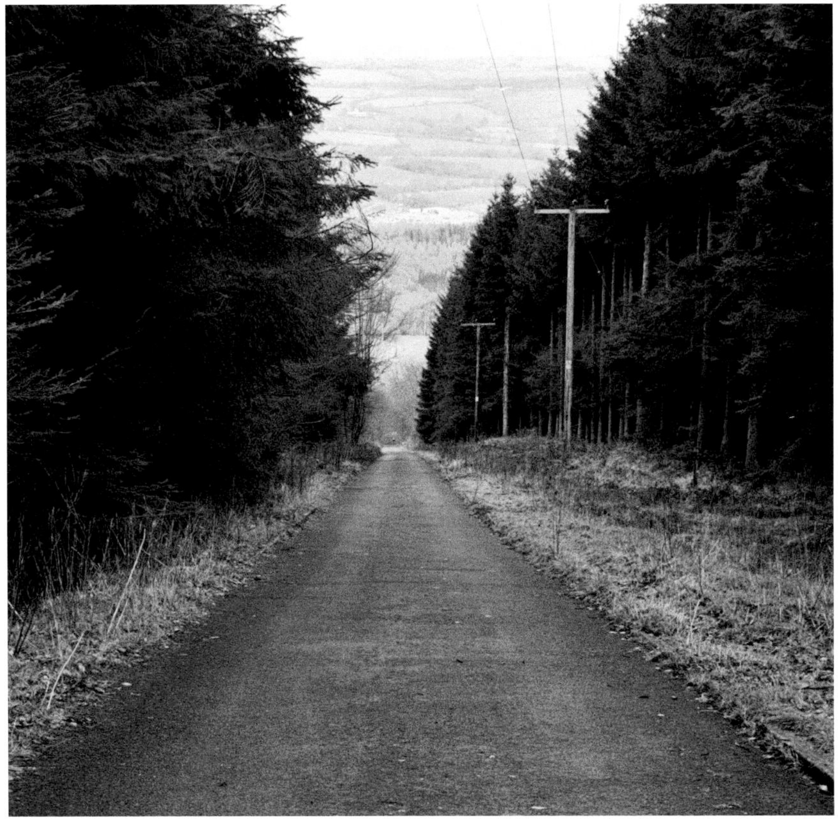

37 | Former incline railway, Brown Clee

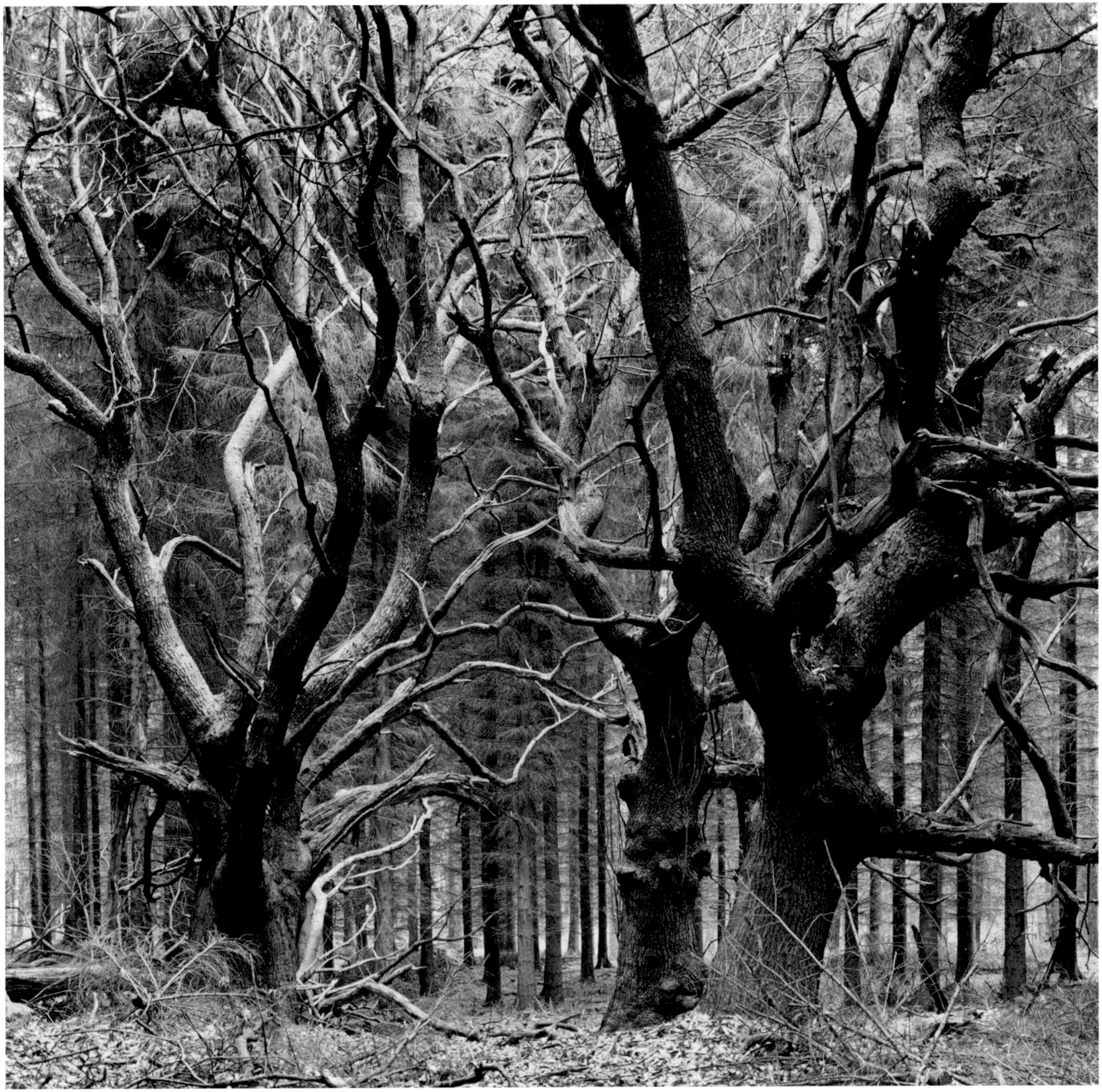

38 | Chestnut trees in conifer plantation, Brown Clee

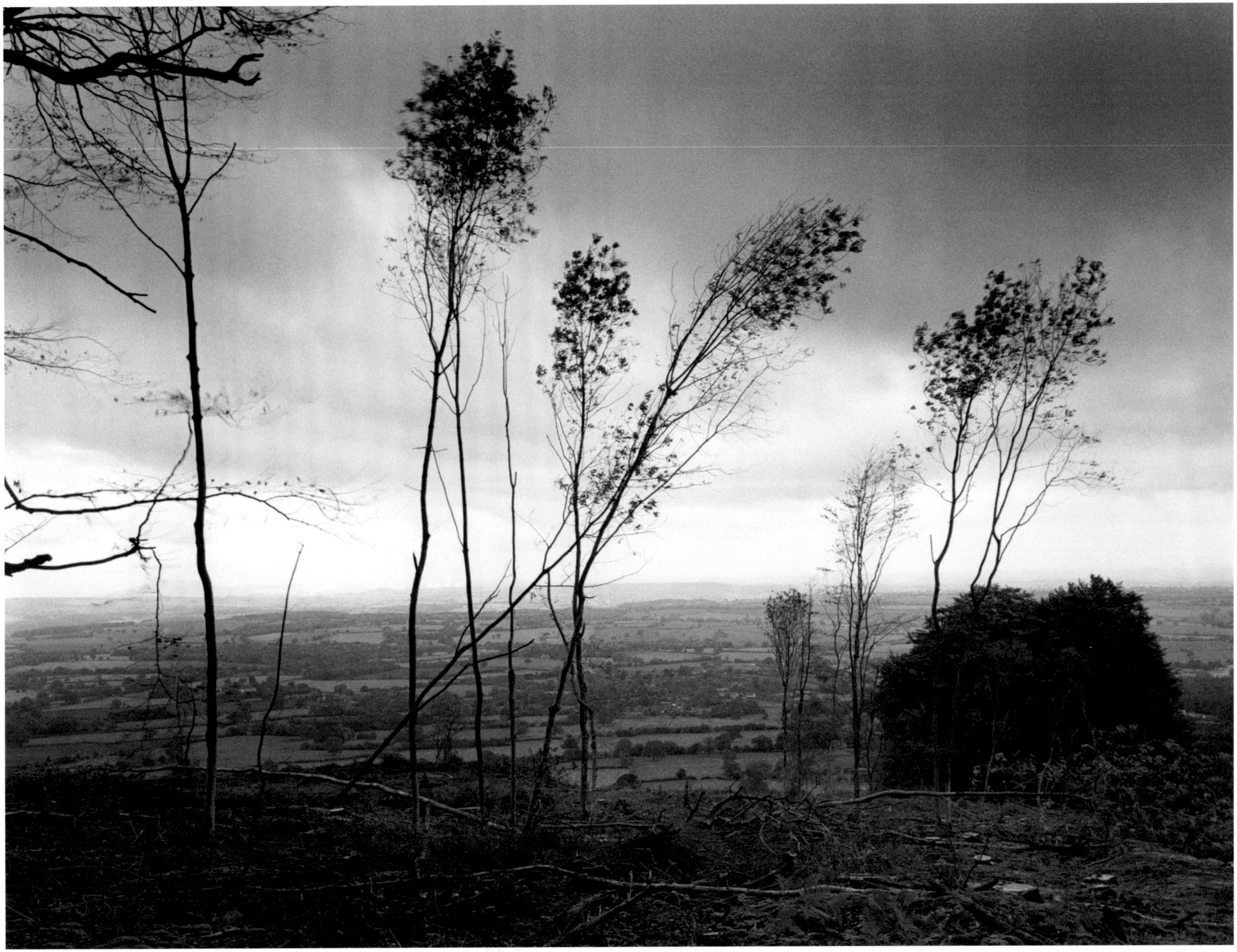

39 | Conifer stumps with birch trees, Brown Clee

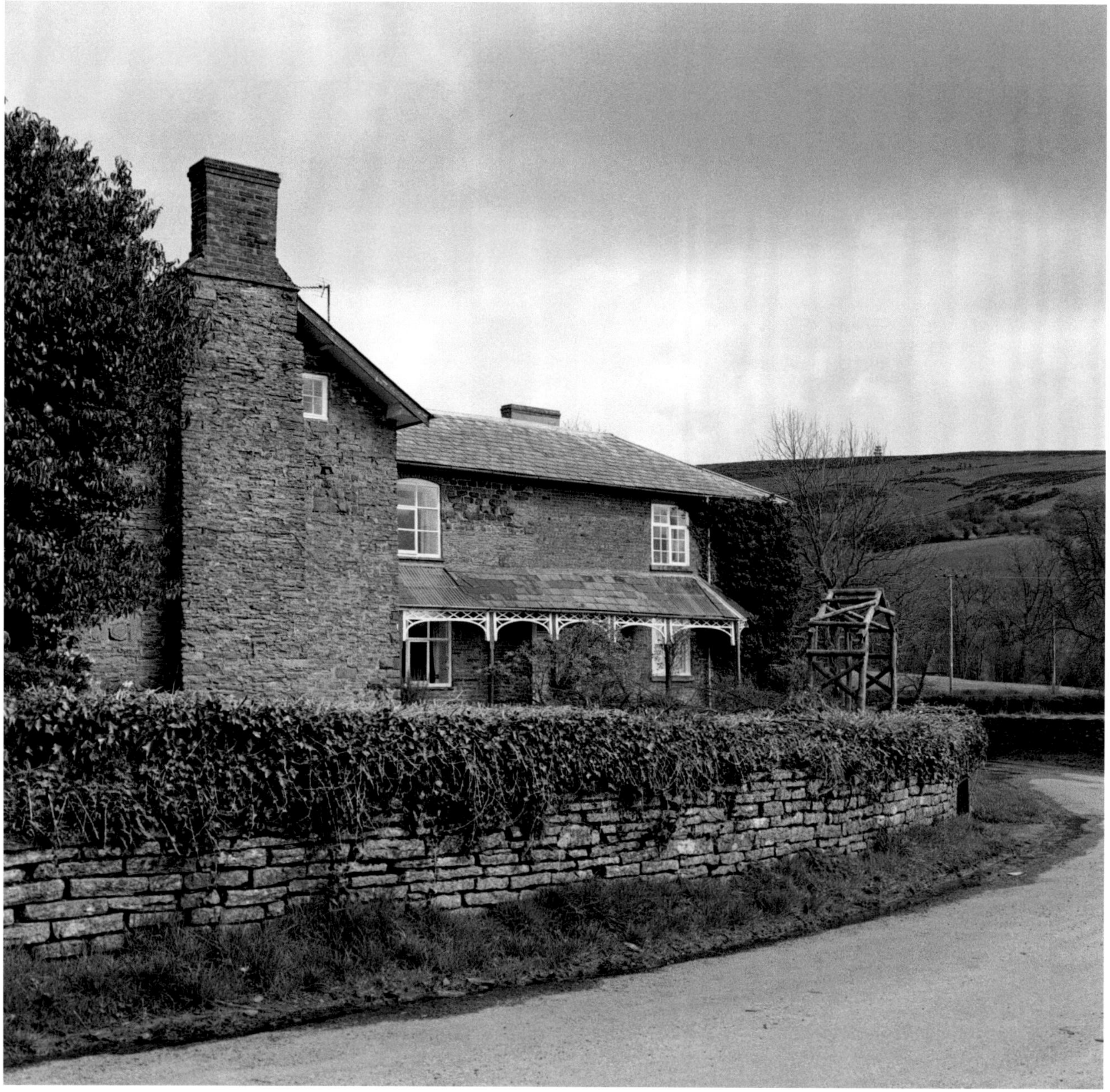

40 | Abdon village looking to Abdon Burf, Brown Clee

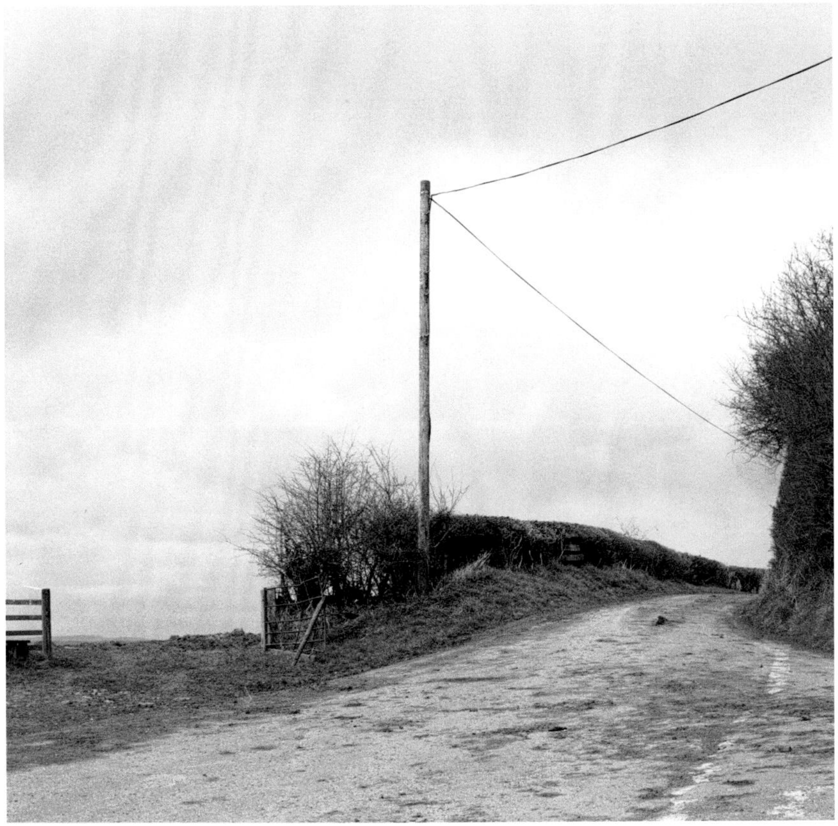

41 | Telegraph pole and stile, Abdon, Brown Clee

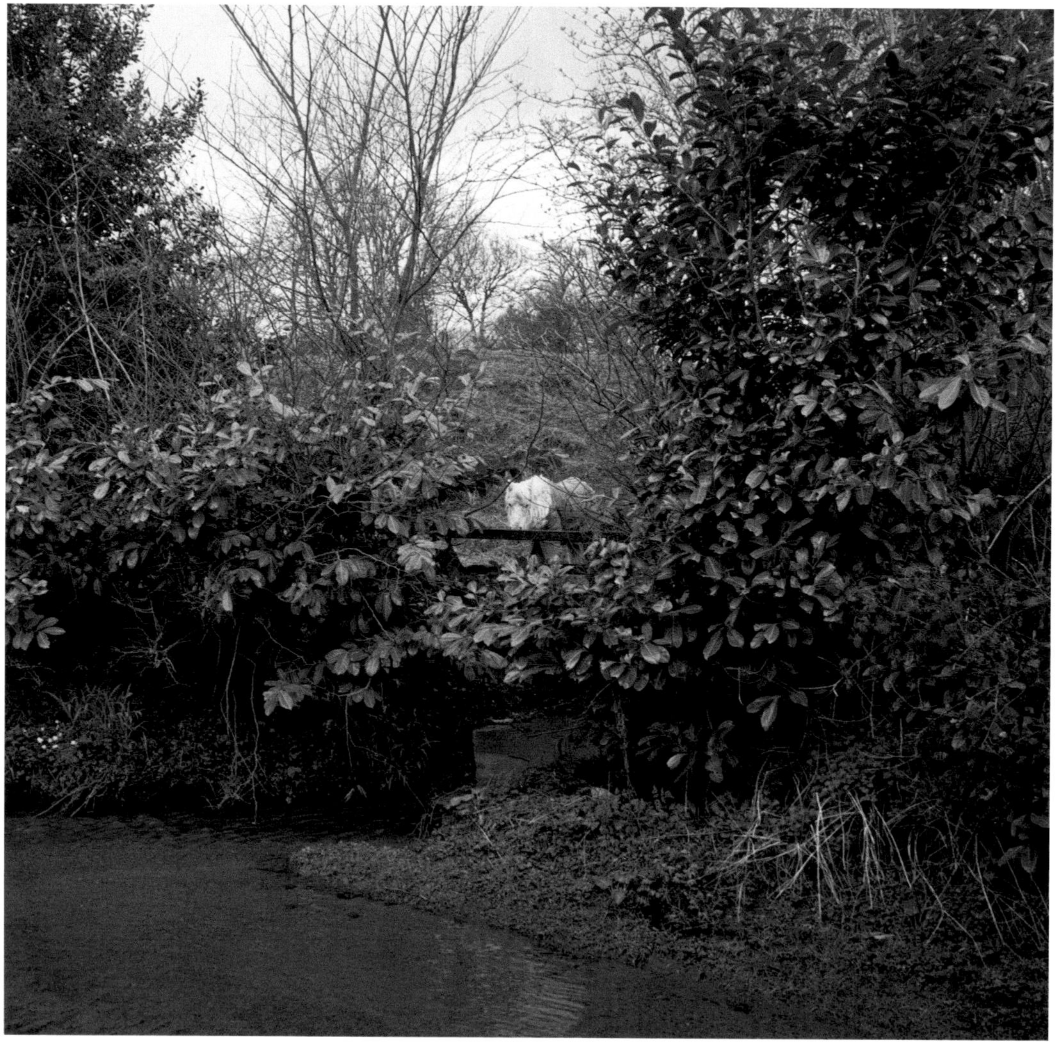

42 | Village ford with pony, Clee St Margaret, Brown Clee

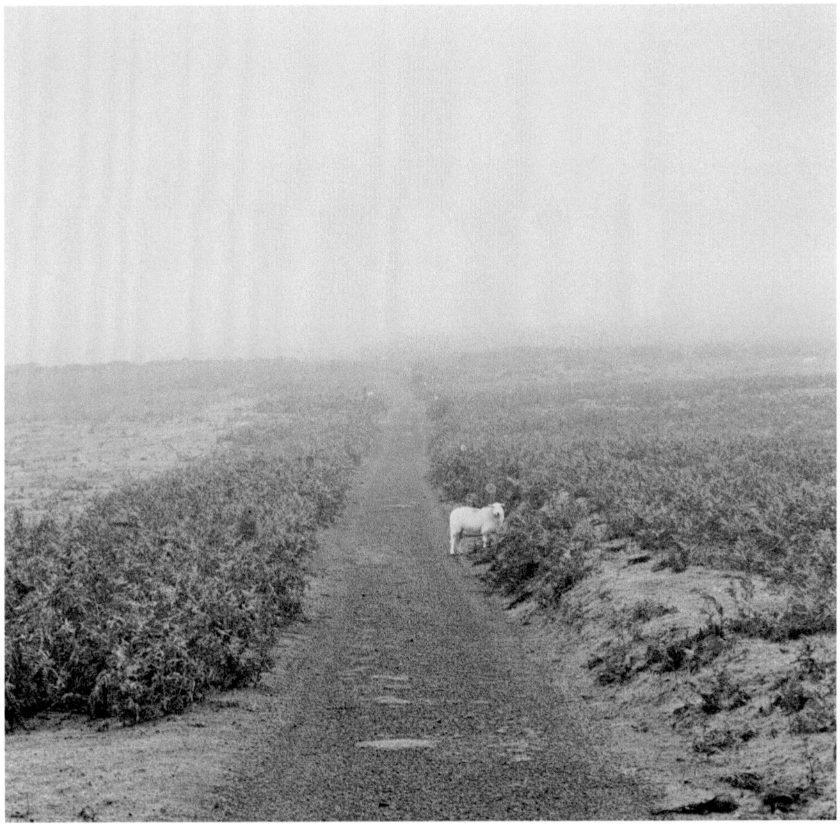

43 | Quarry road with sheep, Brown Clee

Jim Parker

Quarry worker's son,
Brown Clee

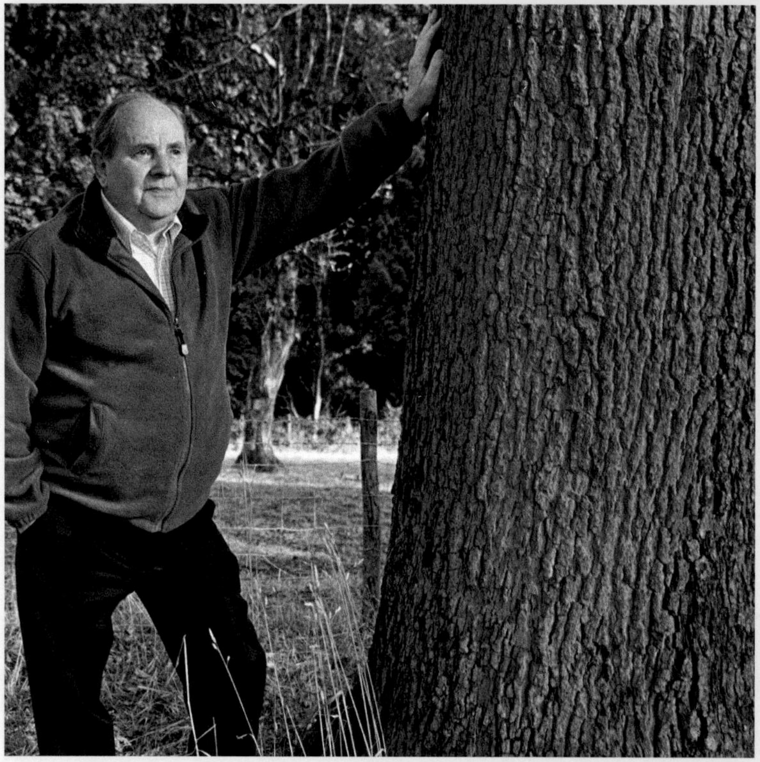

44 | Jim Parker

Dad left school at 13 and went straight to work in the Abdon quarries – this was in 1914. They'd start work at daybreak, and from Abdon it was an hour's walk up the hill to the quarry before he'd even started to swing a big hammer and a shovel. Dad was a 'face-man', breaking the stone up with a 28lb hammer for eight hours a day. And they'd be out in all weathers – it was one hell of a job.

Practically everybody who lived around here worked in the quarry. My grandfather, my three uncles, they all worked there. A lot of them had other jobs as well. If they were smallholders with a few acres of ground, they'd have to deal with the stock before they went up, or work on the land after they'd done a day's graft on the hill. Dad had a big allotment and he'd walk down the hill and do a couple of hours' digging of an evening. They were hard men.

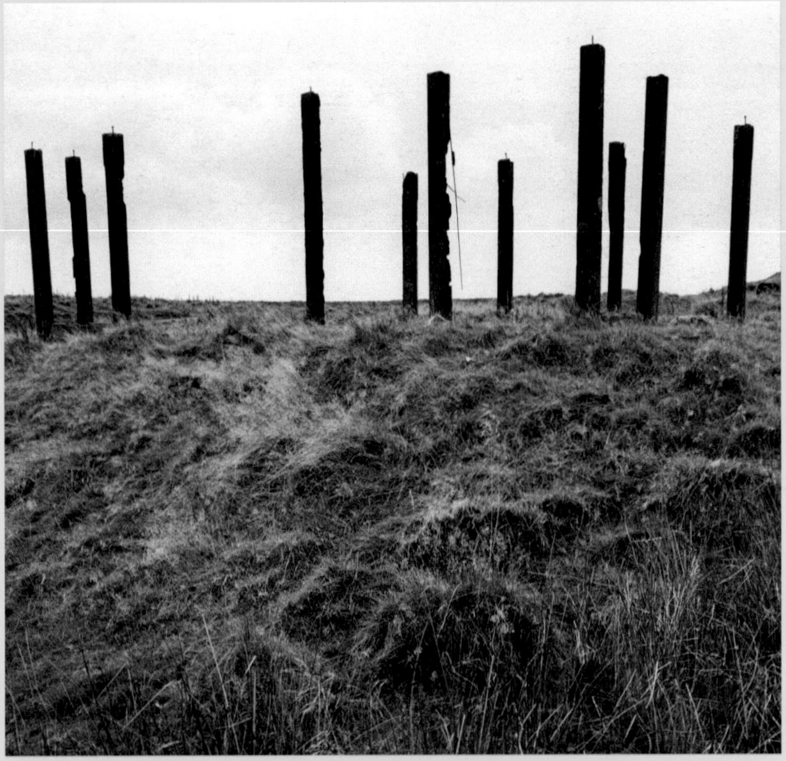

45 | Remains of 'whizz-bang' locomotive shed, Abdon Burf, Brown Clee

People walked to the quarries from all over the area, from as far away as Ludlow and Bridgnorth. Some of them lived rough, in old buildings or anywhere, and used to go home weekends.

In the quarry they'd blast the rock first. They'd drill holes into the face, tamp the black powder in, put the fuse in, seal it with clay, light the fuse – and run like hell. Then it would be broken up by hand into manageable pieces, so it could be lifted into the rail trucks. Then it all went into the crusher.

Dhustone is very hard stone. The newer types working in the quarry would just thrash at it with their hammers. But the old quarrymen would roll a big stone over, and look at the grain; and perhaps with one or two really good bumps on the top it would split open.

The quarrymen wore no protective clothing, nothing whatsoever. Not even gloves. There'd be stone chips flying about, and they'd always have nicks and cuts on their hands and arms. The chaps who were sett-makers – chipping the stone into blocks for paving or building – they used to have metal-mesh goggles; but I never saw anyone else wearing them.

It was a hard life but I never knew the quarrymen to go on strike or have any real problems with their employers. They were on good money. When farm workers were getting 15–25 shillings a week (just under or over £1), Dad was coming home with £5 or £6. They were on piecework – they'd get so much for a truck of stone, and so much for a truck of soil – so the more they did, the more they earned. If they were on a good face that was all stone with very little overburden, they were on a good thing.

The Abdon Clee quarries closed in 1936, when I was 11, but as a kid I used to go up there and roam around, because everybody knew me, and ride around on the 'whizz-bangs' – the little locomotives moving the stone from the quarries to the crusher. They were ex-War Department jobs, from the First World War. I knew the drivers and I used to sit up on top of the engine cowling, with my legs dangling down by the driver's seat. It was great fun.

After the quarries closed, a lot of the quarrymen went to work at the Cockshutford quarries near Clee Burf on the other side of Brown Clee. But the dhustone there wasn't as good as over the Abdon side and that quarry didn't last long. So most of the men came back and worked at the naval ammunition depot they'd set up at Ditton Priors village, down the hill, at the start of the war.

It's very rural around Brown Clee now, but it was an industrial place before the war, because there was the concrete plant and the tarmac plant in Ditton Priors, plus the railway – and the quarries. If the wind was coming down over the hill you could hear the crusher at the top crunching away, even down in the village.

The quarries were all finished by the time I started work – so I drove lorries and coaches most of my life. But I'm glad I never had to work up there on the hill. I never fancied grafting like that.

Maud Massey

Hill farmer,
Brown Clee

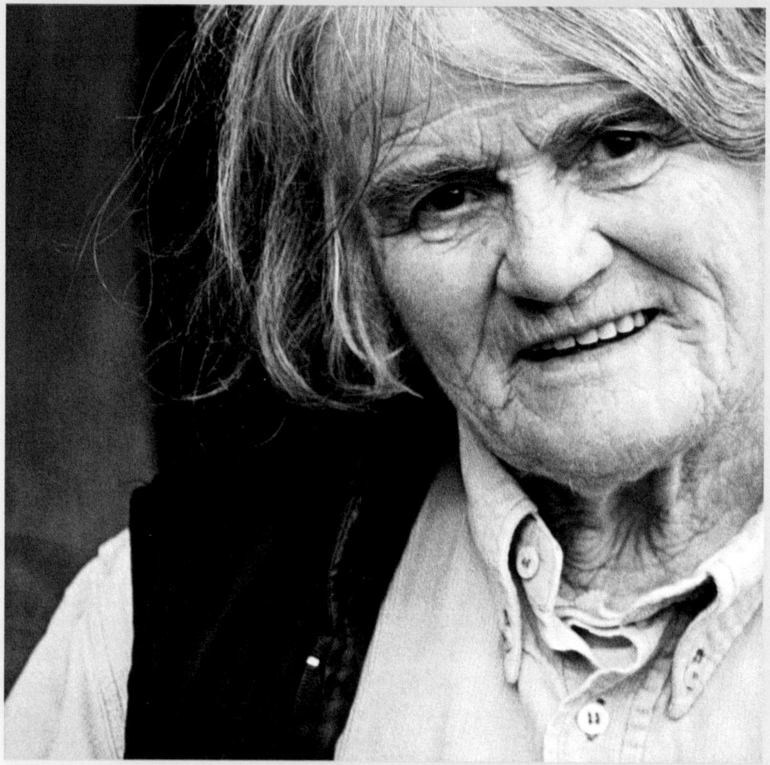

46 | Maud Massey

All my life I have kept stock on the hill, as my father did before me. Before the war, when the quarries were still in operation, our sheep used to lie down on the railway tracks and they were quite often killed or injured.

If we found one injured, we'd carry it home to get it better. Father had two poles, wooden ones, with some sacking in the middle to make a bed. And he and Mum would carry the sheep down, and I used to trot along by them, just a little girl. We'd carry the injured sheep down the rides that Lord Boyne, the landowner, used to drive his carriages round.

When the quarries finished in the 1930s and 40s, we had to look out for the great pools of black tar that they just left up there. When it was hot weather we used to throw sticks down to stop the sheep running on it, because the tar would melt. We had a pony in it once and quite a few times we'd find sheep stuck in it, and they'd be dead.

Most of the war we didn't have too much bother, although there were many planes that came down on the hill. Once a Lancaster bomber crashed up on the top of Abdon Burf. That night I'd gone to a dance in the village, down at Tugford. When we were told there was a plane that had come down, I rushed off on my pony and met some police looking for the spot. They followed me but not carefully enough because one of them – a sergeant – slipped into one of the old mine-pits on the hill, right into the water. Up there it was terrible, there was this blazing plane, and all of the crew lost their lives.

But there was another time – in November 1944 – when I helped rescue somebody. I was 22. It was a foggy, rainy day, and I was gathering up ponies from the hill. I couldn't get them to go their normal way home, over Hay Meadows, and it was nearly dark when I got home. When I arrived, Father said, 'There's supposed to be an airplane come down up there, you have to go back'. So I went back up, but I couldn't find the plane. We rang the Home Guard, but they said it would be hopeless to come at that time of night.

So I went up again at daybreak, and there it was, the crashed Wellington bomber, still smouldering on the Hay Meadows. It had trailed along the ground and left two dead bodies. I looked under a wing and there was a man there still alive. He'd got broken legs, a damaged side and his face was charred. I went and called my father who was half way down the hill, and he went to fetch a little whisky which we took back up the hill. Then Father went to summon the police, and the airforce came and carried the man down in a Landrover.

I had a lovely time growing up on the hill. Best of all I liked riding horses, breaking them in – I used to love the rough work even when they were a bit naughty. I started riding when I was about two, with Dad up on the hill fetching sheep, sitting in front of him. Then he'd just leave me on the horse coming down the hill, with the stirrups dangling and the straps rolled up so you could get your feet in them. Dad would walk down the slope behind, following the sheep.

Going up on the hill now that all the quarries are deserted doesn't feel different but you sort of feel older, because looking back you think: that was a while ago.

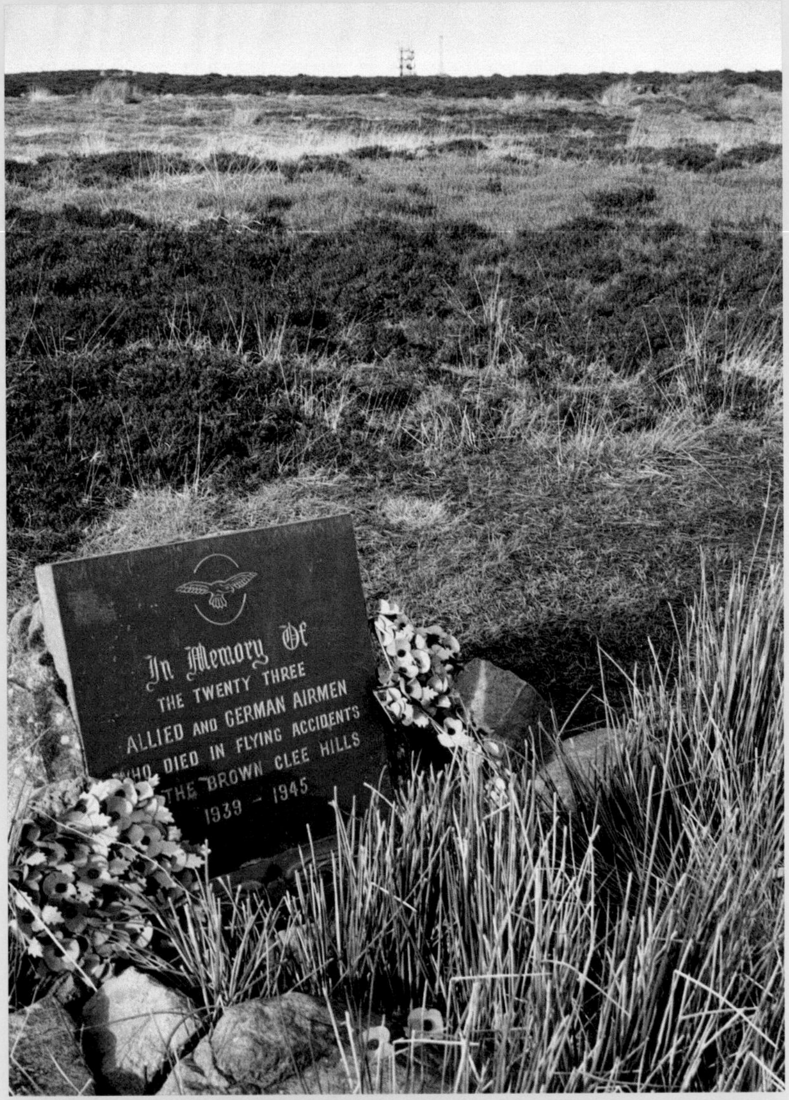

47 | World War II memorial, Brown Clee

Mike Bradbury

Head forester,
Boyne Estate,
Brown Clee

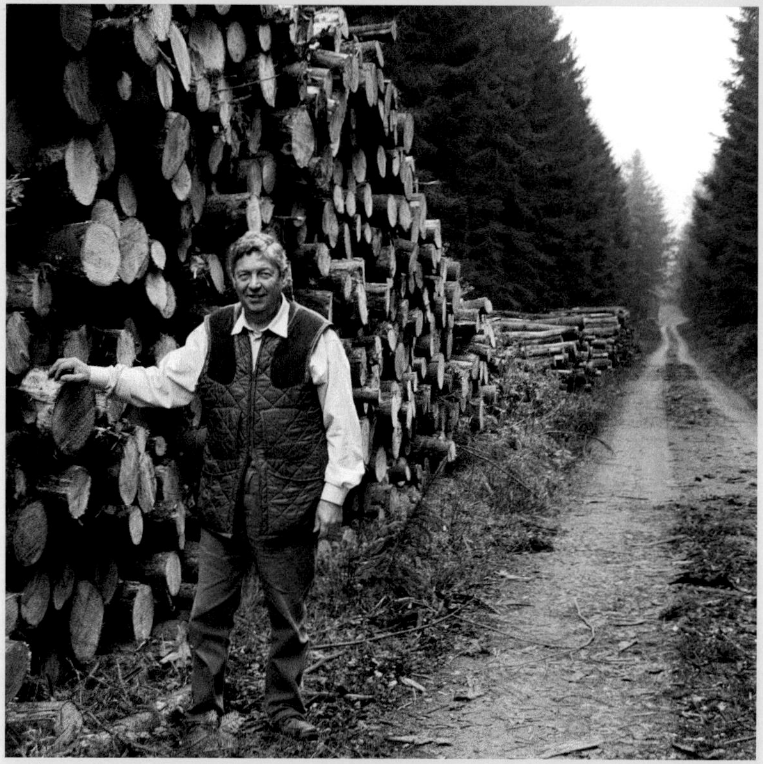

48 | Mike Bradbury

The whole eastern side of Brown Clee has been well-wooded since the 1850s, when Lord Boyne's family first bought the estate. The forest used to go right up to the quarries at the top – but forestry isn't viable up there, it's too high and exposed.

So we moved the forest down the hill a stage during and after the Second World War. That was when some of the older stands of broadleaved trees lower down the hill became incorporated into the forest.

Most of the pools in the woods were created for ornamental reasons, and to create employment for local people – estates used to do that in the 19th century. Of course labour was very, very cheap in those days. There are still parts of a Second World War bomber in one of these pools, Boyne Water. There's an aerial photograph taken in the mid-1970s, which shows the skid marks where the plane hit the ground before going into the pool. The ground obviously took a long time to heal over.

A few years ago we cleaned the pool out and refilled it, and we found bits of metal in there. But the engine is still in the pool – they tell us it was never dredged out. It must be buried deep, we didn't see it.

We clear-fell an area of woodland every year, and we thin the woods out every year, all year. You remove the smaller trees to allow the better ones to grow on. We fell around 7,500 trees a year, but I am also planting nearly 30,000 this year. Clear-felling is all mechanised nowadays. Harvester machines grab the tree, slice it off and cut it into required lengths, before stacking the timber on the side of the path to be loaded onto lorries. We only hand-fell trees that are too big for the harvester to grab, or when we are thinning an area.

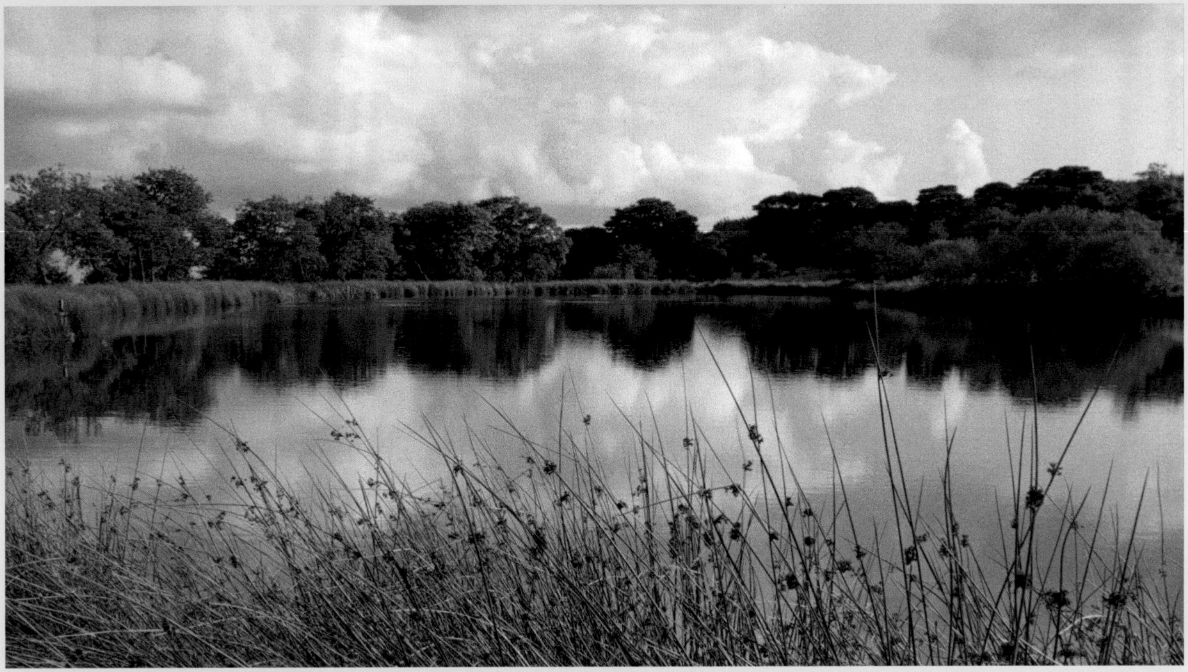

49 | Boyne Water, Brown Clee

When you clear-fell an area of conifers, it can look very bare, there's very little undergrowth. But when you let the light in, it soon explodes again, and all those seeds that have lain dormant for the best part of 30 years just come up. You'll get some conifer seeds; but you get all the other things as well – foxgloves, gorse, briars, bramble and finer grasses.

We aren't over-commercial. We keep and plant a lot of broadleaved trees for landscape interest, and we open up views for walkers. We are generally happy for walkers to go wherever they want, as long as they are causing no damage. I just wave and say 'Good morning'. If they were lighting a fire it would be a different matter. People do occasionally camp on the hill without permission – I come across their campfires.

There haven't been great changes to the quarry buildings in my time here, which is nearly 30 years. But we did make some of them safer by capping a few walls that were loose. The biggest difference is the new communication tower on Abdon Burf. One of the masts is owned by BT and the other one by the Home Office.

It's very satisfying to be able to mould the landscape the way we do. I feel quite at home in the woods, much less threatened there in the middle of the night than I would in the middle of Birmingham.

As for the other Clee Hill, I have been up Titterstone – but very rarely. It's a very different sort of hill, much more open, more rugged and wild. I think the people are different too. More independent, much more likely to settle grievances on their own account. Brown Clee is more an entity; all the eastern slope is under one ownership. Over there it's fragmented, and I think it feels like it.

Di Bryan

Local historian,
Brown Clee

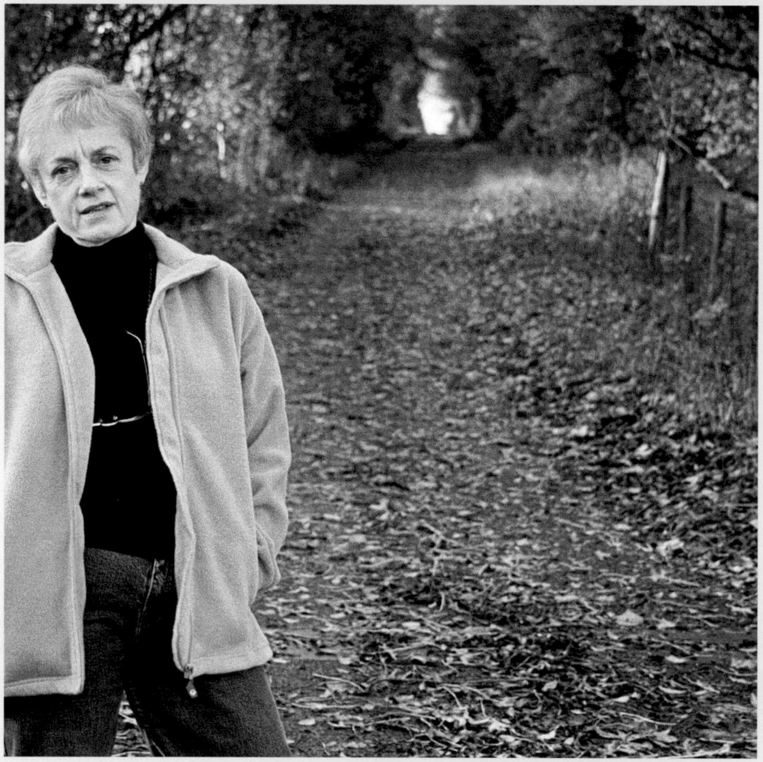

50 | Di Bryan

I was a social worker in Birmingham before I took early retirement and moved to Shropshire in 1998. When we came here I became secretary of our local history group and I have since become fascinated by the history of the hill.

We know there was medieval mining on the summit because there's one reference to the Prior of Much Wenlock giving someone a license to dig coal as early as the 14th century. The whole hill was thickly wooded in the Middle Ages – it was a royal hunting forest. Only the eastern side is wooded now.

I walk up the hill once or twice a month. Getting to the top makes you feel really exhilarated; there's so much of awe and beauty up there. You can't walk anywhere on the hill without seeing bell-pits from medieval and later coal mining, remains of quarrying, even plants that provide evidence of the hill's earlier history.

I can understand people who say it can be eerie on the hill, with all the gaunt ruins on top and the conifer plantations on the eastern side. You peer into these plantations and it's dark – there's nothing underneath the trees, and very few birds that you can hear.

But you have to see the hill for what it is. There's one track we often walk down through the conifers, and all the way down there is dhustone from the quarries that has just been dumped there. I like to think of people coming down this route in Victorian times or later, dropping this stone off as they went, perhaps to make the heavy wagons more manoeuvrable or to stop them slipping on the steep and sometimes boggy slope.

The two Clee Hills, Brown Clee and Titterstone, are very different, even though they are next to one another, have the same geology and a very similar industrial history. The summit of Brown Clee seems somehow cut off and remote from the surrounding villages, which are all medieval in origin. On Titterstone the houses where the workers lived are much more a part of the hill – they were built there because of the industry, and they are much higher up the slope. On Brown Clee industrial history has become archaeology, but on Titterstone, at least on some parts of it, it is still everyday working life.

A lot of the difference between the hills is probably to do with the landowners. The owners of Brown Clee were always as interested in hunting, forestry and agriculture as they were in mining and quarrying. One gets the impression that the people who had Titterstone quarry were simply there to exploit the quarry – building a massive railway from Ludlow, along with their other heavy investments.

Lord Boyne, on Brown Clee, surrounded his big house at the bottom of the hill with beautiful gardens and built carriage drives around the hill, even after the incline railway was built to the quarries. One gets the feeling that carriage drives would not have been quite so important on Titterstone.

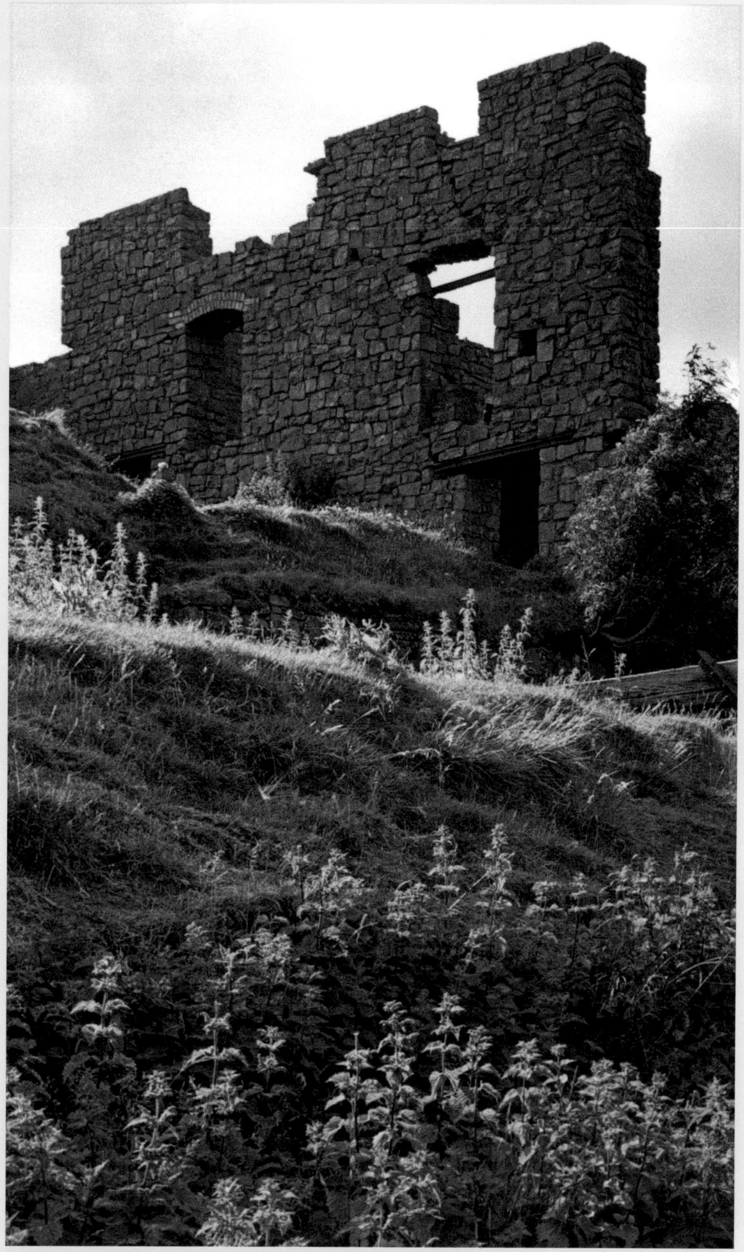

51 | Crusher building, Abdon Burf, Brown Clee

Phil Collier

Station engineer,
Titterstone Clee
Radar Station

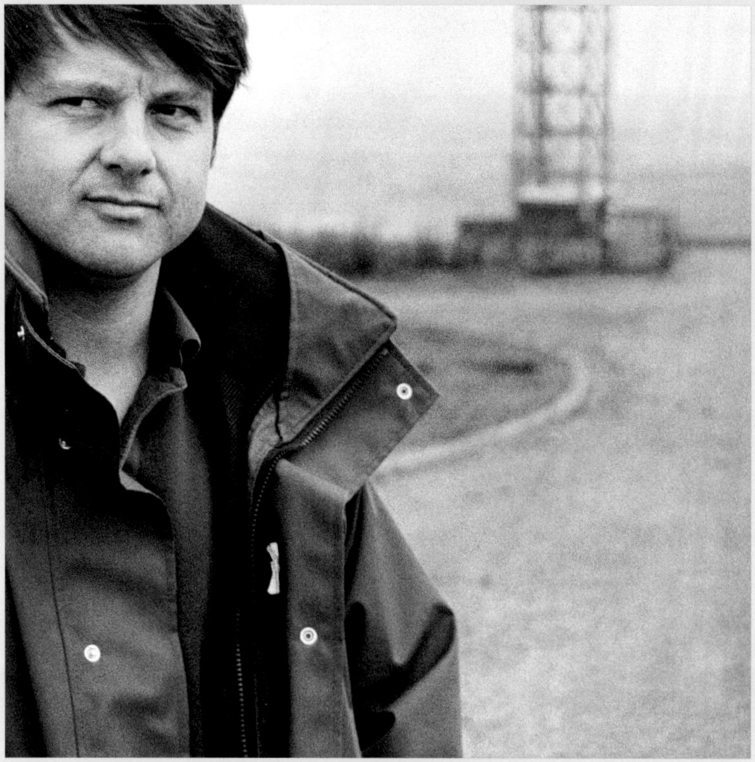

52 | Phil Collier

The work we do at the radar station on Titterstone Clee is a lot less glamorous than you'd think. We send a radar picture of all aircraft flying within about 100 miles of here to air traffic control centres. Controllers can then communicate with the aircraft remotely using our radio masts – the ones here on Titterstone to speak to the aircraft and the ones on Brown Clee to get messages back.

We are quite passive here. The information all goes one way – from us to air traffic control. We don't even know who uses the information we send. We never get any feedback.

We simply maintain the site. General wear and tear, power cuts, that sort of thing. But as the equipment becomes more reliable, there is less to do. There used to be about two dozen people working here, now we just have half a dozen. I'm sure it's going the way of lighthouses. In time this place won't be manned permanently. I'll still be fixing it – but I'll be driving from one station to another.

I love it up here especially in the winter; the way the ice forms on the fences. It's so raw. The temperature quite often drops to minus 10°C. With the high winds, it never snows downwards, it always snows across.

The atmosphere of the place is quite humbling. From up here you have got such a vast view of the countryside, it makes you aware how small you are. But it also makes you feel a bit more alive.

The light is always changing – there is always something going on in the weather. You see little micro-climates, bands of rain moving across, or thunder and lightning somewhere in the distance. You also see a lot of wildlife. Sparrow hawks and kestrels hover at about the level of our windows, even though they are actually quite high off the ground.

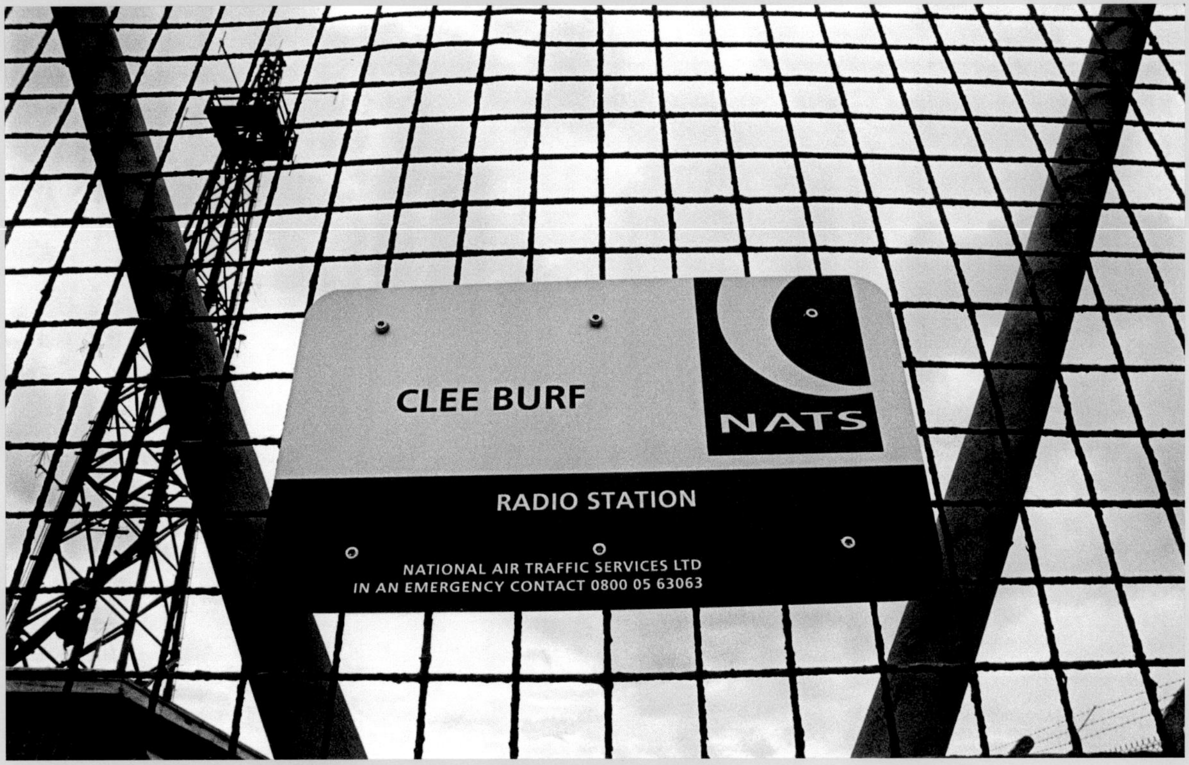

53 | Radio mast, Clee Burf, Brown Clee

With our bird's-eye view we can see people riding across the common, or walking on the hill. Occasionally people come up and ask if they can paraglide off the top. There are also parties of schoolchildren, perhaps on field trips. It always seems to be raining when they come and you see them standing around huddled up in their little cagoules.

We also get the joy-riders, who come up at night to dump their cars and set them on fire. People always say it's kids from Birmingham but no one really knows. I guess word gets around that it's the kind of place you can wreck a car and not get disturbed.

We don't really have any dealings with the other people who use the hill, like the farmers. We have our compound and that's it. Sometimes the sheep get locked inside for a few hours. It's quite useful, they keep the grass short. The farmers never seem to want to come up and reclaim them. But the sheep are smart, they just walk across the cattle grids. They always get out eventually.

There has been so much land-use here over the centuries, with things always changing and going out of use. The radar station itself has been on this site since 1963 and it is constantly evolving. Eventually it will become derelict and people will come up here and wonder what the buildings were all used for.

David Stockwell

Manager,
Clee Hill Quarry,
Titterstone Clee

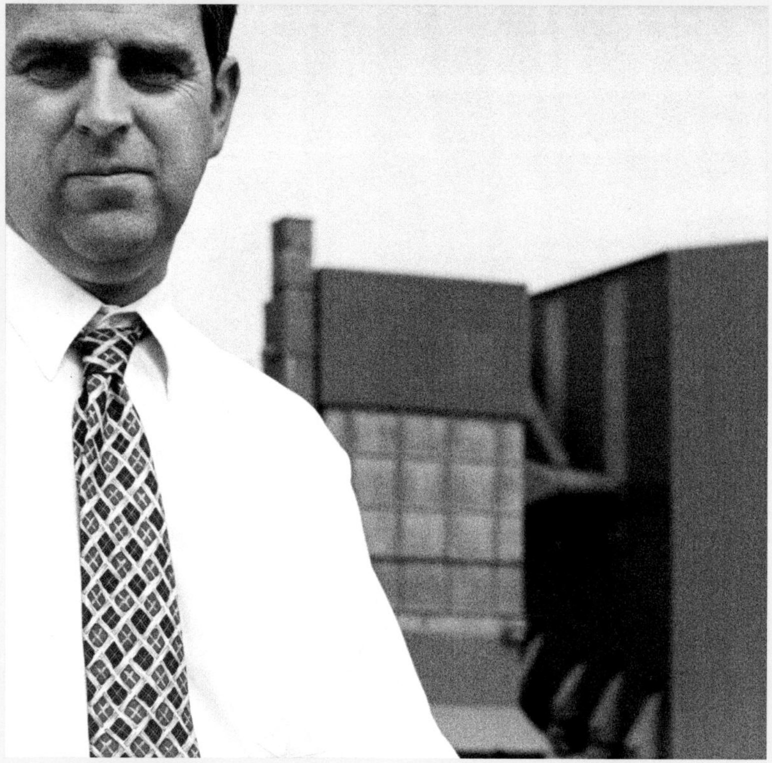

54 | David Stockwell

The stone we quarry here is basalt – known locally as dhustone, from the Welsh word *dhu* meaning black. It is exactly the same stone as was taken out of the old quarries at the top of Titterstone last century.

The quarry is surrounded by common land, and before we blast we set sentries all around the perimeter to make sure the area is clear. At present, touch wood, we haven't had any problems with people straying in when we are about to fire.

At other times we get the occasional walker. There is a public bridleway that comes off the main road, runs down the back of the coating plant and out to Titterstone summit, and people do have a tendency to get lost. I have to go flying into the quarry once in a while, to tell people to pop back over the fence because they are close to being pulverised. Unfortunately all the 'Keep Out' signs are wrecked. People like shooting at them with air rifles.

Quarrying is a dangerous industry, but nowadays we try and minimise the number of accidents. The last accident here was about four years ago – someone slipped and twisted his ankle. It was very different last century. They used to scale down the faces on ropes and lever the stone off with crowbars, and the quarry face would be a sheer drop of 60 metres.

Mechanisation has changed everything. If you go back to 1900, there were 2,000 men working in the quarries on Titterstone Clee and they produced over 400,000 tonnes a year. Today, I've got just 18 men and we produce 325,000 tonnes. Our stone is used mainly in construction – foundations, that sort of thing. A proportion goes into tarmac. It's a very hard, very abrasive stone. Its main value is that it doesn't break down at all.

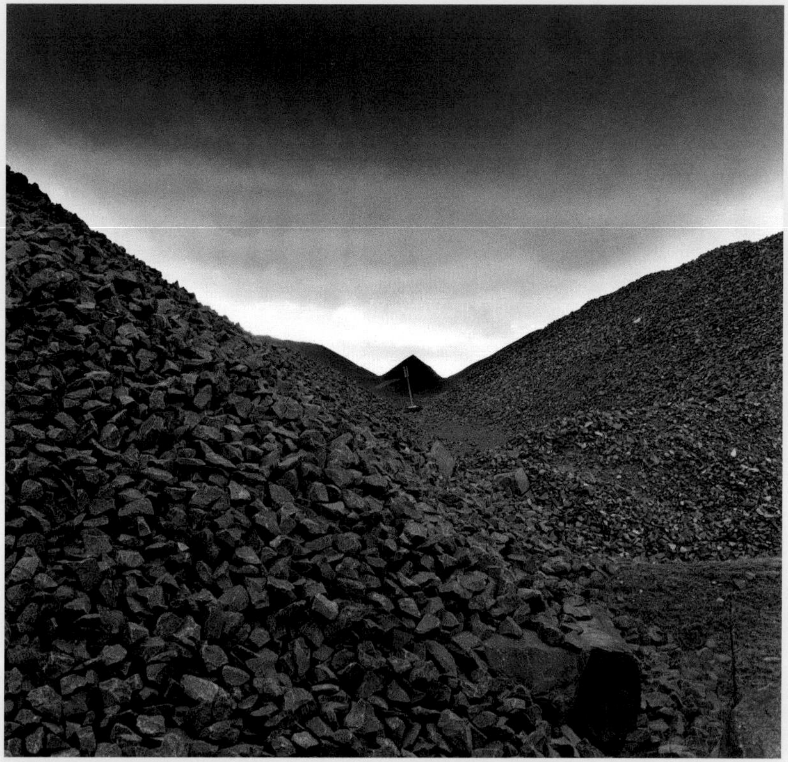

55 | Quarried dhustone, Clee Hill Quarry, Titterstone Clee

Our current planning authorisation is valid until 2048, and there are basalt reserves here to take us up to that point at the current production rate, and beyond. But there are limits. The hill is not all made of basalt. The basalt is extruded through the overlying limestone and sandstone and is really only in one area of the hill.

The Clee Hill commoners have grazing rights around the quarry and they are entitled to come in to gather up their sheep. We have no problem with that, but they have to abide by the health and safety legislation. They have to come to reception to make themselves known, and wear hard hats and high-visibility clothing. The commoners understand that – or at least most of them do.

The only problem we occasionally have is people fishing in the old flooded quarry within our perimeter. The water gets very deep in there, and there is no suitable standing point around the edge. If they fall in, there's no easy way out. God help them if they get on the western side because there's a 30 metre face.

We are getting more and more dumped cars down here. Whenever we find one, we contact the police. The strange thing is, these cars are rarely reported stolen. When the police contact the last owner, he usually says he sold it to someone in a pub two weeks ago. Unfortunately you can't leave these cars lying around. Oils, petrols, burnt rubber, burnt materials – it's all hazardous waste. We have to dispose of them at our own cost. It's annoying.

The hill is quite unreal in some respects. It's in its own little micro-world. Everybody knows everybody else. The majority of people in Clee Hill village today had parents and grandparents who lived here, and many of them would have worked in the quarries in the 19th and 20th centuries.

Because there were so many people who used to work here, Clee Hill had its own little community. If there were 2,000 men working in the quarries, think how many families used to be here. A lot of those people migrated from Ireland, Wales and all over Britain. So the village always had a very strong sense of community and it seems to have retained that. The rest of South Shropshire is very rural, just farming. Clee Hill really stands apart.

Roddy Yapp
Hill farmer,
Titterstone Clee

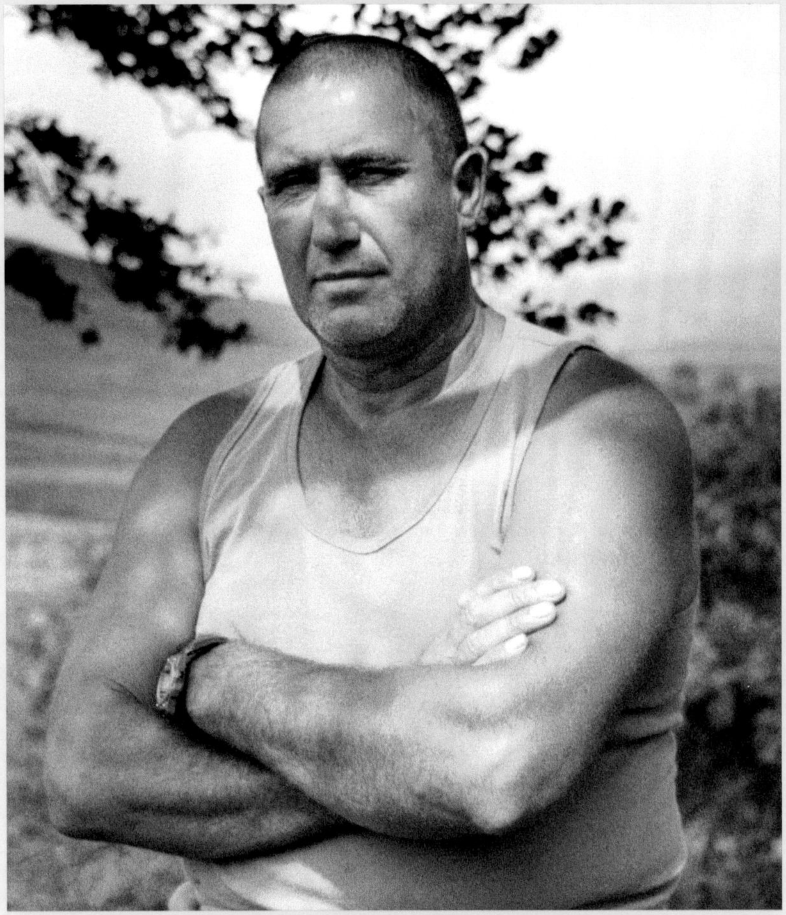

56 | Roddy Yapp

When I was younger, one lot of my grandparents – and later my auntie – lived in the house we live in now, right on the top of Clee Hill, and I used to stop here a lot then, because I never attended school a great deal, and it was always very convenient having places like this because nobody could ever find you.

I left home when I was 14 as I didn't get on so well with my dad. He used to like a drink and sometimes I'd be the loser when he'd had a drink. So I went to live with anyone who'd have me – with my gran, or aunties.

After my auntie left the house, it became derelict, and we used it as outbuildings for stock. We had sheep up the stairs and everything. But eventually, ten or twelve years ago, me and my wife got the house and built on it. We've got no electric. The lights are from a generator, and we've got a small windmill and batteries that we charge up at night.

Our family have always been part and parcel of Clee Hill. I've cleared sheep off this common since I was about 10 years old, back in the 1960s. Three or four times a year, they'd clear the sheep for lambing, for tupping, for dipping and occasions like that. We'd start at Clee Hill village and go right over the top and end up at Callow Lane on the other side. There'd be as many as 20 people driving the sheep across, and 40 dogs, and the majority would be on horseback.

It'd be an occasion. They'd funnel them into Callow Lane, and drive them to the top of the lane where

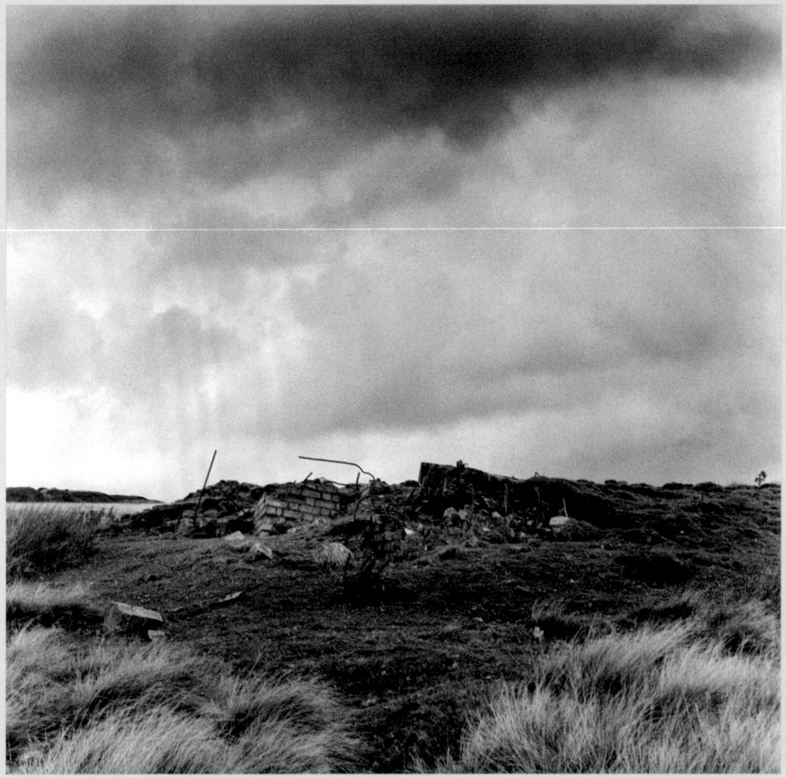

57 | Collapsed quarry structures, Whatsill, Titterstone Clee

there was a pen, and then alternate farmers would catch their stock out. They'd have jugs of cider there, and all the farmers would be helping. We do still do it, but there's nowhere near the numbers involved now.

My gran, when she lived here, she said once when the weather wasn't too good she went four weeks without seeing anyone else – apart from the immediate family. Four weeks! Not even people walking. I used to feel terrible claustrophobic when the fog was down. And it's a crazy place to live if you don't like the fog. But you do get used to it.

It's only a matter of time before someone is killed on Clee Hill. In the last four years, I have seen three old mineshafts collapsed in. You are talking about a hole that's straight down, 10 feet round, and 50–60 feet deep, if not deeper. They are capped with a brick dome, that's all. They aren't filled in. Either the dome gives way, or the wall further down gives way; and then it all falls in. Not a month ago, I had to go and tell some boys on BMX bikes what they were riding back and forth over the top of.

Another danger is the old quarry at the top of the hill, with sheer straight-down drops of over 100 feet. I've been up there, in thick fog, on a horse that's a bit fresh, and you've got them big white radar domes going *bubububububub* with the wind – and the horse is looking at that and going sideways towards a 100-foot drop. It makes the hairs on the back of your neck stand up.

It's a place of beauty, here. But I'm convinced a lot of folks who come into the area would like to see the old workings pulled down, and all the slack tips levelled and grassed over. We've had battles with people wanting to put up parking areas, and picnic areas with benches and things for people to sit on. They should leave it as it is.

I find it quite pleasant being so high up and remote, to be fair. Time could stand still up here and it wouldn't matter to a soul. I've got no peer pressure to do anything I don't want to do. Also I find it easier dealing with horses, dogs and kids than with adults, because with animals and kids what you see is what you get.

As I get older I find myself stopping more and looking at the view, and looking at different things, whereas 20 year ago I would have thought, so what? But when you have been into the centre of Birmingham or somewhere like that, you really appreciate what you've got. There's no comparison between somewhere like that and here – none whatsoever.

Nic Adams

Landlord,
The Kremlin Inn,
Clee Hill village

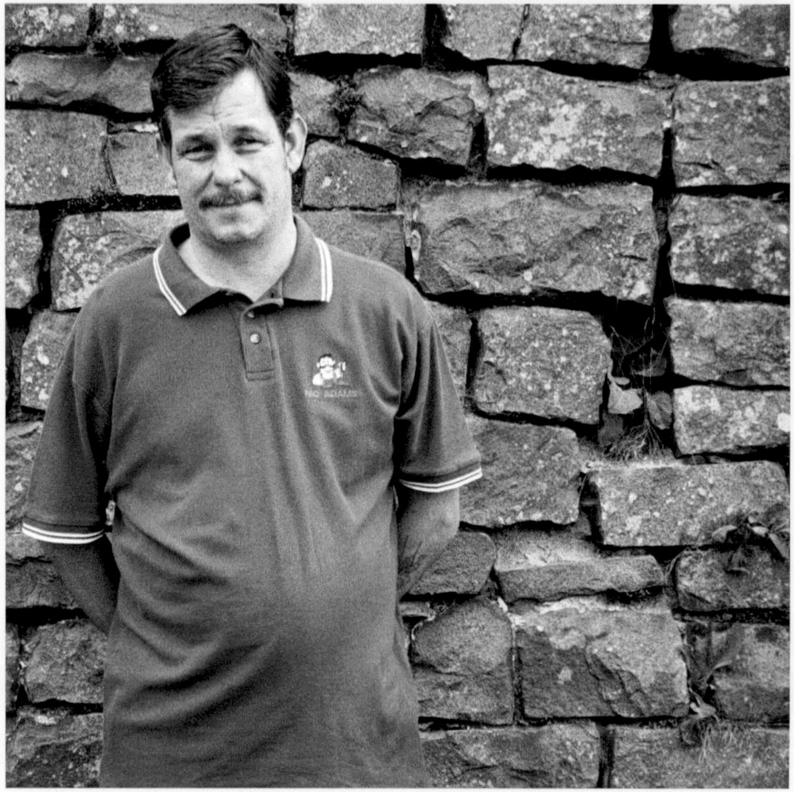

58 | Nic Adams

Most of the locals in my pub are farmers, but a lot of people round here keep a few sheep – not just the farmers.

It's common land on Titterstone Clee and you need turn-out rights. I've got turn-out rights, but I don't want any sheep. I see enough in the car park, bloody things. They crap everywhere, people get it on their shoes, and they walk into the pub here and get it on the carpet.

This pub's called the Kremlin because when we first come here in the late 80s, we used to get Radio Moscow coming through the jukebox when there wasn't any music playing. We also got it on the telephone and the television, beamed off the radio mast on top of the hill – because from here to the Urals there's no high ground. It was quite spooky. Then they moved the mast to the other side of the hill and we don't get it any more.

The Kremlin used to be the quarrymaster's house, so I believe, before it was a pub, but it has been a pub for about 100 years. It was designed for the quarry workers and the local farmers, and it's still a working men's pub, definitely. We still have the darts, dominoes, and quoits teams in the bar. But in the summer we also get a lot of people from Birmingham and the Black Country who come to look at the views.

Clee Hill people definitely think of themselves as different from Ludlow down the hill. There always used to be a rivalry. Clee Hill lads would go down to Ludlow and there'd be fights, and Ludlow lads would come up to Clee Hill when there was a dance at the village hall, and they'd be going through the windows. It's not been as bad since we come here, but it used to be pretty rough. They still have trouble at the football club discos here sometimes.

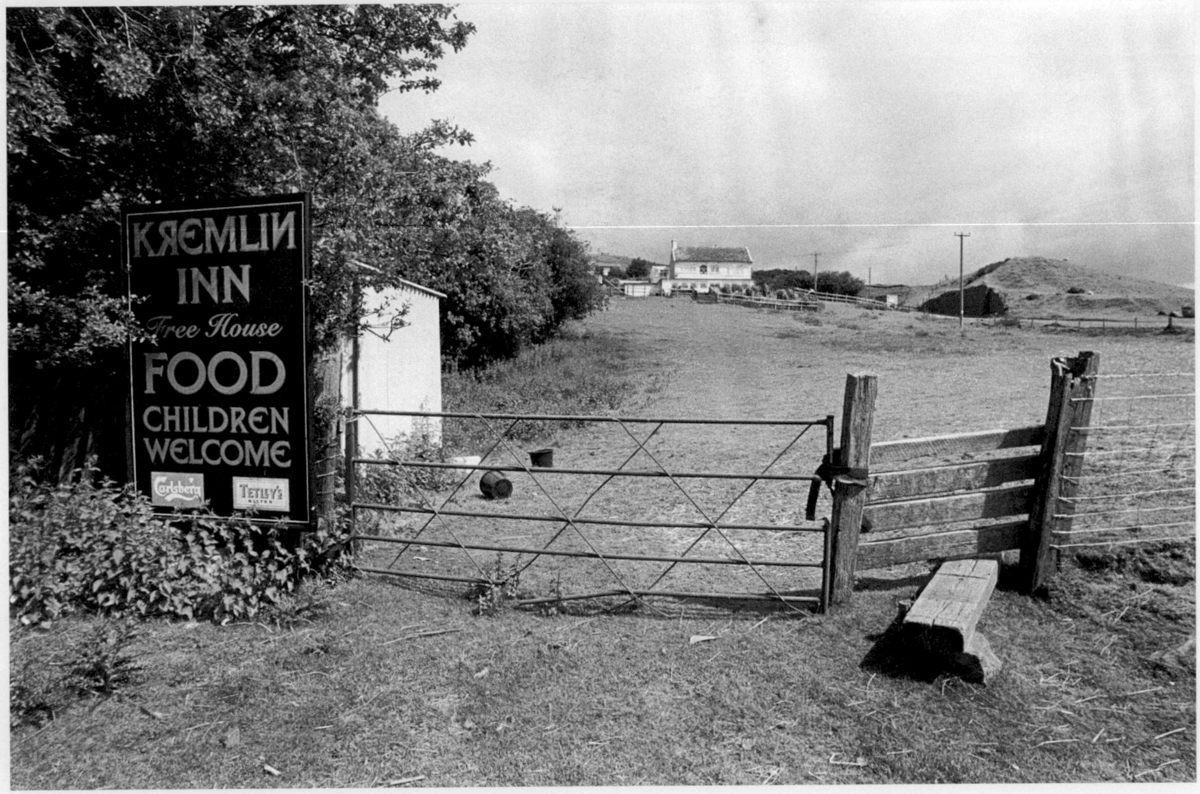

59 | The Kremlin Inn, Clee Hill village, Titterstone Clee

Everyone knows everyone in Clee Hill. Everyone knows everyone's family and everyone's business. They're all inter-related. You've got to be careful what you say – it's 'Oh, he's my uncle' or 'He's my cousin'.

Most of them would never move off Clee Hill. It's amazing. Me and my wife have moved all over the country, and I've never been anywhere where there are so many people that have never lived anywhere else – and don't want to live anywhere else. I don't know why, they are just Clee Hill born and bred. Not just old people, but young people in their 30s as well.

I don't think you'll see the locals going up and looking at the old quarry remains too much. But we get a lot of walkers who come in here and say, 'How do we get to the Three-Forked Pole?' – and all that sort of thing. So the history brings people round here, that's for sure.

This is the second highest pub in England at 1,400 feet, after the Tan Hill Inn in the Pennines. Sometimes we get cloud all down below in the valley, and it's like looking out over the sea – it's beautiful. It can also be foggy as hell up here for days on end and it's horrible then. That's the worst part about Clee Hill. Drizzly rain and fog, it's horrible.

List of Photographs

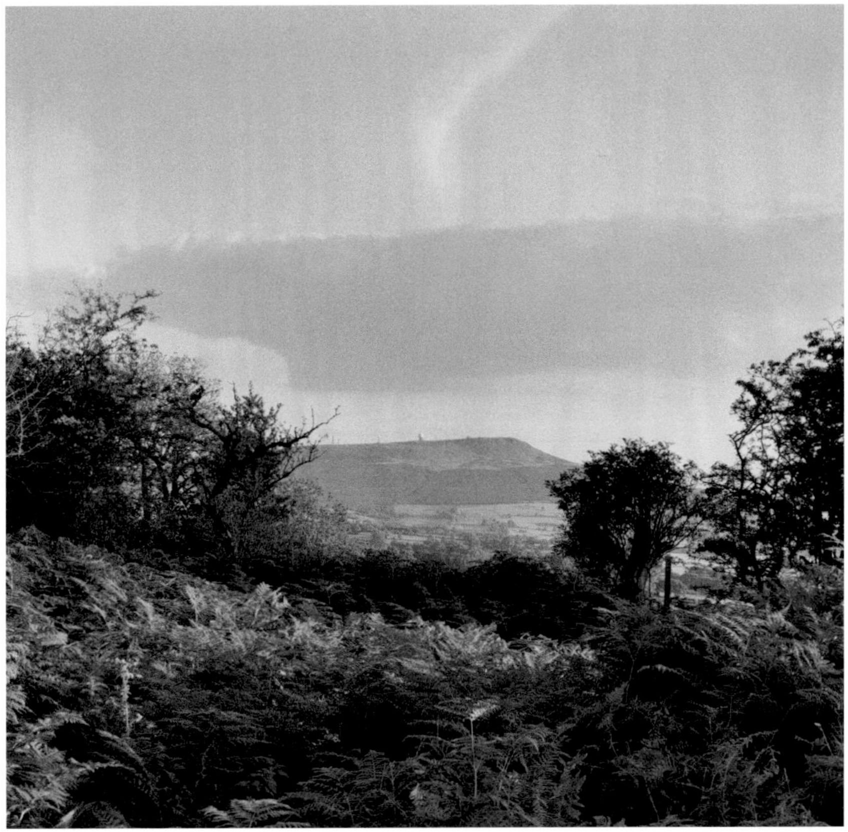

60 | Titterstone Clee from Brown Clee

First published in 2005 by
Greyscale Books
Email: greyscalebooks@pobox.com

Designed by Esterson Associates
Email: simon@estersonassociates.co.uk

Printed in duotone and bound in a limited first edition of 800 copies by Balding + Mansell, Norwich

Quarry Land was supported by grants from Arts Council England and from South Shropshire Arts

ISBN 0-9541878-1-4

Quarry Land was exhibited at the Midlands Arts Centre, Birmingham (March–May 2005), the Assembly Rooms, Ludlow/Ludlow Festival 2005 (June–August 2005) and at other venues

Copies of *Quarry Land*, and of Simon Denison's first book *The Human Landscape* (Greyscale Books, 2002, ISBN 0-9541878-0-6), can be obtained directly from the publisher

For further information, please contact greyscalebooks@pobox.com

All images in *Quarry Land* are available as signed, archivally-processed, hand-printed, limited edition, silver-gelatin fibre prints, or as signed, limited edition, archival carbon pigment prints on art paper

For further information please contact Simon Denison directly at simondenison@pobox.com, or see www.simondenison.co.uk

Images with captions marked by an asterisk (*) appeared in *The Human Landscape*